《云南少数民族非纸质典籍聚珍·丝帛素书类一》编委会名单

国家民文出版项目库项目
民族文字出版专项资金资助项目

云南少数民族非纸质典籍聚珍

云南省少数民族古籍整理出版规划办公室◎编

丝帛素书类一

和六花◎主编

云南出版集团
云南人民出版社

图书在版编目（CIP）数据

云南少数民族非纸质典籍聚珍．丝帛素书类．一 / 云南省少数民族古籍整理出版规划办公室编；和六花主编．-- 昆明：云南人民出版社，2020.1
ISBN 978-7-222-16922-7

Ⅰ．①云… Ⅱ．①云… ②和… Ⅲ．①少数民族—古籍—汇编—云南 Ⅳ．① K280.74

中国版本图书馆 CIP 数据核字 (2018) 第 260396 号

出 品 人：李　维　赵石定
责任编辑：金学丽　马　滨
封面设计：马　滨
责任校对：沈正德
民文校对：和丽宝（纳西文）　王明富（壮文）
责任印制：代隆参

云南少数民族非纸质典籍聚珍·丝帛素书类一
YUNNAN SHAOSHU MINZU FEIZHIZHI DIANJI JUZHEN · SIBO SUSHU LEI YI
云南省少数民族古籍整理出版规划办公室◎编
和六花◎主编

出版　云南出版集团　云南人民出版社
发行　云南人民出版社
社址　昆明市环城西路 609 号
邮编　650034
网址　www.ynpph.com.cn
E-mail　ynrms@sina.com
开本　889mm × 1194mm　1/16
印张　23.5
版次　2020 年 1 月第 1 版第 1 次印刷
印刷　重庆新金雅迪艺术印刷有限公司
书号　ISBN 978-7-222-16922-7
定价　560.00 元

云南人民出版社
微信公众号

如有图书质量及相关问题请与我社联系
审校部电话：0871-64164626　印制科电话：0871-64191534

概说

我国是一个统一的多民族国家。在漫长的历史发展进程中，各民族创造并积累了丰富多彩的历史文化，留下了浩如烟海的古籍。这些古籍资料，从不同的角度记录中华各民族的社会进程、历史走向和文化内涵，从不同侧面反映各民族祖先的智慧、文明成果和气质风貌，是中华文化的重要组成部分，是文化传承的独特载体，是中华民族多元一体格局的真实映射。少数民族古籍是其中不可或缺、独具特色的重要部分。云南素有“民族文化博物馆”之美誉，各民族先民创造了卷帙浩繁的书面文献和难以计数的口传文献。这些少数民族古籍涉及的语言文种多种多样，记录的内容博大精深，载体形态更是纷繁复杂，有记载历史时期官方盟誓、功绩、先贤德行、颁赏、封诰等的金石铭刻，有描绘先民生产生活景致和认知的岩画，有刻写了经书、经文和神灵造像的石刻，有绘制于麻布之上的各民族信仰的神灵造像，有用铁笔刻写在贝多罗树叶上的贝叶经，等等。这些便是本套丛书所要收集、采录的少数民族非纸质典籍。

一

中国少数民族古籍（以下简称少数民族古籍），是指中国55个少数民族在历史上用各自的语言文字形成的文献典籍、碑刻铭文和口头传承资料等。其内容涉及政治、哲学、历史、宗教、军事、文学、艺术、语言文字、地理、天文历算、经济、医学等领域。本套丛书收集、采录的少数民族古籍的时间范畴一般以1911年为下限，但由于各民族的历史特点和古籍存世情况差异，根据各民族古籍的实际情况，有的可以延伸到1949年。

少数民族古籍是中国传统文化的重要组成部分，是古籍学、文献学的重要研究对象。过去，传统研究未对此作出全面、系统的阐述，直到20世纪80年代，随着各级各类民族古籍工作部门的建立，民族古籍工作迎来了春天。1981年中共中央在《关于整理我国古籍的指示》中指出：“整理古籍，把祖国宝贵的文化遗产继承下来，是一项十分重要的、关系到子孙后代的工作。”1984年，国务院在转发《国家民委关于抢救、整理少数民族古籍的请示》的通知中强调：“少数民族古籍是祖国宝贵文化遗产的一部分，抢救、整理少数民族古籍，是一项十分重要的工作。”根据指示精神，从国家到地方都建立了相应的民族古籍工作部门，全面开展少数民族古籍的抢救保护、整理出版工作。我国少数民族古籍工作以“救书、救人、救学科”为己任，取得了丰硕的成果。然而，这项工作也面临着重重困难，走得异常艰难。随着社会日新月异的发展，少数民族古籍资源和古籍人才流失态势日趋严峻，少数民族古籍学科的发展又相对滞后，基础理论研究十分薄弱。诸如，中国各少数民族古籍种类众多、卷帙浩繁，对于少数民族古籍的分类至今仍无定论。对“民族古籍”的界定，是一个非常重要的问题，观点众说纷纭①。这里，我们无意对此做系统梳理，只为明确少数民族非纸质典籍收录的范围。

在少数民族古籍抢救保护、整理出版工作中，特别是1997年以来，围绕《中国少数民族古籍总目提要》开展的全国范围内的少数民族古籍整理工作中，我们习惯性地将民族古籍主要分为两大类：一是有文字类；二是无文字类。有文字类的民族古籍又包括三个子类：一是用各少数民族文字及少数民族古文字记载的历史文书和历史典籍；二是用汉文记载的有关少数民族内容的古代文献典籍；三是用少数民族文字和汉文记载的有关少数民族

---

① 李国文在《云南少数民族古籍文献调查与研究》（民族出版社2010年版）一书的前言中对学界关于“民族古籍”的理解和界定做了较为系统的回顾。近年，也有相关研究做了一些讨论，观点几乏善可陈。

内容的碑刻铭文。无文字的民族古籍主要是指各少数民族在历史上口头传承下来的具有历史和文化价值的各种资料[①]。在《中国少数民族古籍总目提要》实施过程中，鉴于少数民族古籍文献载体形式的不同，又将少数民族古籍细分为书籍类、铭刻类、文书类和讲唱类四类予以收录[②]。其中，书籍类全面收录少数民族在历史上形成的具有古典装帧形式的书册。铭刻类收录石碑、摩崖石刻、墓志、鼎彝、哀册、金属刻、竹木刻等碑刻铭文。文书类收录各类告示、契约、传单、函告、函件、账单、抄件、公约、规章、执照、档案、书信、柬帖等文献资料。讲唱类则收录少数民族口头传承的有关民族起源、民族迁徙、文明起源等具有历史文化价值的神话、传说、故事、歌谣等。依据少数民族古籍文献载体产生的四分类法，用于《中国少数民族古籍总目提要》各民族卷的编撰是符合客观实际且行之有效的。与此同时，因此项工作涉及面广、持续时间较长，这个分类法影响力较大。但是，依据古籍的载体形式对民族古籍加以分类，可否将“文书类”单独归为一类尚可斟酌。何谓“文献载体”？《辞海》中对于“载体”一词给出了五层解释，其中一个“指承载知识或信息的物质形体”。顾名思义，“文献载体”就是文献的物质载体，纸、绢帛、布匹、木头、树叶、兽骨、石头、金石器物、兽皮等等都可作为文献载体。“文书”一词起源甚早，早在汉晋时期的史籍中即已出现，是指以文字为主要方式记录信息的一种书面文书，按其性质可分为对公文书和对私文书，各类告示、契约、传单、函告、函件、账单、抄件、公约、规章、执照、档案、书信、柬帖等皆属文书。从这个层面来说，文书是依照文献内容界定的概念。在云南少数民族古籍中，同为文书，也有不同的物质载体形式，有书写在纸上的，有凿刻在砖石上的。

此外，乌谷先生《民族古籍》一书对民族古籍的概念及其分类颇具代表性，他认为：“民族古籍就是指曾经在中华人民共和国疆域范围内生活过的各少数民族或正在生活着的各少数民族在历史上遗留下来的一切用文字、具有某种文化含义的符号（文字的雏形）及口头语言记录下来的文化载体。这种文化载体可分为四大类型，即原生载体古籍、金石载体古籍、口碑载体古籍和书面载体古籍。”[③]按照乌谷先生的分类，各民族在历史上留传下来的以竹简、布帛、纸张为载体的各种历史文献，包括用各种民族文字书写出来的书籍、

① 国家民族事务委员会全国少数民族古籍整理研究室：《中国少数民族古籍总目提要·纳西族卷》“序言”，中国大百科全书出版社 2003 年版。

② 国家民族事务委员会全国少数民族古籍整理研究室：《中国少数民族古籍总目提要·哈尼族卷》“序言”，中国大百科全书出版社 2008 年版，第 10 页。

③ 乌谷：《民族古籍学》，云南民族出版社 1994 年版，第 6 页。

档案、文书、诏令、户籍、契约、谱牒、信札、告示、乡规民约等都归为书面载体古籍。而在众多的分类法中，铭刻类（或称金石载体古籍）、讲唱类（或称口碑古籍）按载体形式作为单独的一类没有太多的争议。但“铭刻类”和“金石载体古籍”因提法不同，内涵和外延产生了很大的差异，铭刻类涉及的物质载体更为宽泛、全面，不局限于金石器物，涵盖了石刻、竹木刻、骨刻、摩崖、器物等，铭刻类实质上已涵盖乌谷先生所界定的书面载体古籍和原生载体古籍的一部分，但“铭刻类”强调的是古籍的书写方式，而非载体形式。“金石载体古籍”这个类目的界定又略显狭隘，未将骨刻、竹木刻等载体形式囊括其中。乌谷先生虽另外界定了“原生载体”这个类目，“原生载体是指在一个民族的文字形成之初，用于记事表意被赋予某种特殊涵义的实物或符号。……我国各民族在自己的历史上都曾先后留下了大量有关刻木记事、结绳记事、实物记事等生动翔实的原生载体古籍。”[①]从这个概念来看，将骨刻、竹木刻归入原生载体古籍一类显然不合适。

综上所述，因中国各少数民族所处的环境不同、历史发展进程各异，少数民族古籍的载体形式多种多样，有的数量稀少却异常珍贵，有的历史上有过却早已佚失。用一种或者几种载体类别对琳琅纷呈的中国少数民族古籍作分类，难度巨大，难免挂一漏万，概括不够全面。我们选择以“非纸质”作为切入点，除了纸质载体以外的，具有有形实物载体的云南少数民族古籍都是我们收录的对象，意在将散布在各地图书馆、博物馆、档案馆等馆藏机构的以及散藏民间的，长期未公之于众的，又具有重要历史文化价值、文物价值和科学研究价值的云南各少数民族非纸质载体古籍汇编成册，公开出版发行。

二

云南是一个多民族聚居的省份，人口达5000人以上的世居少数民族有25个，除回族、水族、满族3个少数民族已通用汉语外，其余22个少数民族使用着26种语言（有的民族使用两种或两种以上语言），其中14个民族拥有23种文字或拼音方案（有的民族使用两种或两种以上文字），并留下了卷帙浩繁的民族古籍。据统计，云南散藏民间的藏文古籍、纳西东巴古籍、彝文古籍、壮文古籍、傈僳族音节文字古籍、白文古籍、普米族韩规古籍、傣文古籍、瑶文古籍等计有10万余册（卷）。其他如哈尼族、苗族、拉祜族、佤族、景颇族、布朗族、布依族、阿昌族、怒族、基诺族、德昂族、水族、独龙族等虽无本民族的古老文字，

① 乌谷：《民族古籍学》，云南民族出版社1994年版，第10页。

但他们靠口耳相传传承本民族历史文化，口传文献丰富多彩，创世史诗、迁徙史诗、叙事长诗、神话、传说、祭祀歌、劳动歌、生活习俗歌等数以万计。此外，有古老文字的民族中尚有大量口传文献流传。云南少数民族口传古籍达4万余种，内容涉及政治、哲学、法律、历史、宗教、军事、文学、艺术、语言、文字、地理、天文、历算、经济、医学等领域。

云南少数民族古籍储量巨大、历史悠久、载体多样，其中不乏非纸质典籍。依据现有资料来看，云南25个世居少数民族都或多或少拥有一些非纸质典籍。每一个民族都曾经经历过或正在经历着无文字的历史阶段，为便于沟通交流、传辞达意，随之萌芽了一些可用于记事表意的“实物语言”或“符号语言”，如结绳记事、刻木记事、树叶信等原生文化载体。在特殊文化场阈中，这些原生文化载体被赋予不同的象征意义，随着人类社会的发展，特别是文字产生后，原生文化载体在群体中的实用价值逐渐被淡化，有的甚至消失在了历史长河中。但在无文字民族中，这些原生文化载体的实用价值已远超其文化和文物价值。原生文化载体是否能纳入民族古籍的范畴，至今仍众说纷纭。鉴于云南各少数民族留存至今的原生文化载体数量不多，且新近发现者居多，族属难辨、释读不易，本书未做收录。在目前所知的十余万册云南少数民族古籍中，基于各民族分布区自然环境各异，历史发展进程各有轨迹，传统文化各具特色，民族古籍的载体可谓琳琅满目，布匹、竹木、兽骨、兽皮、金石器物等都在不同的历史时期成为不同族群古籍的承载体。这里，我们大体介绍一下非纸质典籍数量较多、载体较具代表性的几个民族的古籍情况：

1. 纳西族典籍

目前已知国内外收藏的东巴古籍有1000余种（内容大体相同的算为一种）3万余册，俗称“东巴经”，多数为图画象形文字写本，部分为图画象形文和哥巴文掺杂写本，极少数为纯哥巴文写本。其以宗教典籍为主，亦包括用东巴文书写的文书、铭刻和纳西族口耳相传的口头文献，内容涵盖社会历史、语言文字、哲学宗教、风俗习惯、文学艺术、天文医学等多方面，被誉为“纳西族古代社会的百科全书”。按其内容可分为祈福延寿类的《远祖回归记》《献牲》《神鹏和署争斗的故事》等，禳鬼消灾类的《鲁般鲁饶》《董术战争》《创世纪》《白蝙蝠取经记》等，丧葬超度类的《杀猛鬼和恩鬼，高勒趣招父魂》《人类迁徙的来历》《马的来历》等，占卜类的《大地上卜卦之书》《用巴格图占卜》《占梦之书》等，涉及舞蹈、医药、民歌等的《东巴舞谱》《医药之书》《民歌范本》等，以及独具地域特色的丽江市宁蒗彝族自治县油米村的阮可东巴经。

纳西族非纸质典籍中，最具代表性、使用最广泛、储量较多的，有绘制于木头之上的木牌画和布匹之上的卷轴画。木牌画是一种历史悠久的原始绘画艺术，是东巴艺术在萌芽阶段的作品，大多应用于大型祭祀活动。木牌一般长约60厘米、宽约10厘米、厚约1厘米，内容依照东巴画谱所记载的为准，按祭祀功能可分为神牌、鬼牌、门牌、还债牌、诅咒牌等。图像造型奇特，形貌古朴，线条粗犷，笔法豪放，自然流畅，具有先民原始艺术的特点。卷轴画，纳西语叫“普劳幛”，是东巴用矿物质颜料绘制于土布上的神像画，是东巴绘画艺术跨入发达阶段而趋于精熟的作品，有长卷、多幅和独幅等多种。每幅卷轴画主要画一尊大神或护法神，表现某个神祇及其所居的神界，用于东巴教仪式中，悬挂于神坛正上方，不同仪式所挂的神像不尽相同。具有代表性的卷轴画有东巴教教主东巴什罗像、东巴教大神依古窝格、战神优麻、阳神董神、阴神术神、萨依威德、神路图等。其中，神路图是东巴卷轴画中最原始、最有代表性的巨作，一般宽16~30厘米、长约15米。画卷分段连续描绘地狱、人间、天堂三个部分，绘有360多个人、神、鬼及70多种奇禽怪兽，被称为我国美术史上最长的直幅长卷，享有“古代宗教绘画第一长卷”之誉，具有较高的文化和艺术研究价值。神路图的内容、性质、用途大体一致，但因载体材质、颜料、绘画技法等不同，每一幅神路图都有独特的艺术风格。

2. 壮族古籍

壮族有自己的语言文字，壮语属汉藏语系壮侗语族壮傣语支，分南北两大方言。壮族文字在先秦时期即已萌芽，隋唐时期，壮族先民即用汉字记壮语，效仿汉字六书的构字方法创制了方块壮字，称“土字”或“土俗字”，并用古壮字来记录民间故事，书写经文、家谱、碑文、账务等，一批方块壮字古籍流传至今。古壮文古籍，壮语称“师摩”“师多在”“师雅”等，“师”壮语意为“书籍”，多抄写在用纱皮树树皮制成的纱纸上，或是用嫩竹、构树皮制成的者卡土纸上。壮族古籍种类广、数量多，有记录摩教仪式、经文、教义的《摩经布洛陀》《摩荷泰》《麻仙》《德傣掸登俄》等，有反映朴素世界观和价值观的叙事长诗、古歌，如《盘古歌》《卜伯》《摩则杜》等，有民间七言叙事诗《毛洪》《董永》《舜儿》等，亦不乏展现绘画艺术的《鸡卜经》及宗教绘画“莱摩”，内容涉及历史、语言、文学、艺术、哲学、宗教、天文、历算等众多方面，可谓博大精深、绮丽多姿。

壮族的非纸质典籍以岩画、骨刻书和绘画典籍较具代表性。一是岩画。今壮族分布区尚存数百处摩崖石刻。据现有考古资料，今壮族分布区有众多的原始刻绘艺术遗存，虽难于明确界定这些考古遗存的族属，但壮族先民是这些绘画遗存的创作者、拥有者之一是确信无疑的。分布在文山壮族苗族自治州境内最具代表性的岩画，有麻栗坡大王岩岩画、丘北黑箐龙岩画、砚山卡子岩画、广南弄卡岩画、西畴蚌谷狮子山岩画等10余处，占地约5430平方米，有170幅400多个图案。二是骨刻书。云南壮族先民在器物、兽骨甚至身体上刻绘图案的历史由来已久，至今仍在部分地区传承使用，其中以壮族的骨刻历算器最为著名，文山壮族苗族自治州民族宗教事务委员会即在境内发现58块骨刻。骨刻，壮语称“甲巴克”“瓦甲巴”，意为刻在骨片上的图纹符号、书籍，是原始先民推算日历、占卜的器具。兽骨上一般刻有人物、桌子、棺材、植物、弓箭、动物、干栏、太阳纹等图像，是一种兼具审美和记事功能的图像文字。三是神像画。壮族神像画众多，类型多样、作品丰富，隐含借“神”避邪的世俗观念，审美态度与情感交织。依据其内容、形制、用途，大体分为摩教神图长卷、宗教挂图和占卜绘画三类。其中，摩教神图长卷是摩教特有的宗教神图之一，由摩教祭司传承使用；绘于壮族自制土麻布上，形制为长卷竖幅，分栏作画，多用于丧葬仪式、祭扫仪式等。

3. 傣族古籍

傣族有本民族文字。傣文古籍多为刻本、写本、稿本和抄本，有贝叶古籍和纸质（绵纸、构皮纸）古籍两种，形制一般为梵夹装、经折装、线装，主要流传于西双版纳、德宏、保山、普洱、临沧、红河等州市的傣族地区。按内容大致有宗教类的《朗丝奢不仙宰》《杀鸡祭水神祷辞》《祭谷魂词》《招魂词》等，政治历史类的《泐史》《孟连宣抚史》等，文学艺术类的《巴塔麻嘎捧尚罗》《兰嘎西贺》《厘俸》，以及天文历法类、农田水利类、医药类、理论专著类、军事武术类、语言文字类、译著类等。

傣族的非纸质典籍载体多样、数量众多，最具代表性的便是傣族的银器、贝叶经书和绘画典籍。其中，贝叶经是最具代表性的非纸质典籍。贝叶经，傣语称作“坦兰”，是用民间制作的铁笔刻写在经过特制的贝多罗树叶上而成的。此外，傣族的壁画、布画等非纸质绘画典籍也较有特色。

4. 彝族古籍

彝族有自己的语言和文字。语言属汉藏语系藏缅语族彝语支，可分为东部、西部、南部、北部、中部、东南部六大方言区。彝族有自己古老的文字，汉文古籍称其为“夷经”“爨文”“罗罗文”等，现统称老彝文，每一个字形代表一个字义，并有不同写法。现存的老彝文有1万多字形，常用的有1000多字。历史上，彝族先民用老彝文撰写了卷帙浩繁的文献典籍和数量众多的金石铭刻，内容涉及政治、军事、哲学、宗教、历史、地理、语言、文字、文学、艺术、天文、历算、医药、卫生等方面。近现代流行于彝族地区的彝文古籍主要有纸书、皮书、布书、骨书、岩书、瓦书、木牍、木刻、金石铭刻、印玺等载体形制，其中纸书占绝对比例，包括抄本与木刻印刷本两种。现存彝文古籍达2万余册（件），手抄本较多，少数为木刻印刷本。云南彝文古籍可分为滇南彝文古籍、武定禄劝彝文古籍、撒尼彝文古籍、阿哲彝文古籍、宣威彝文古籍、罗平彝文古籍、北部彝文古籍七类。较具代表性的有传统宗教礼仪典籍《吾查》《们查》《指路经》《祭龙经》《祈雨经》《鲁资楠道》《脑斯古》《招魂经》《尼布木司》等，著名文学作品有《阿诗玛》《尼迷诗》等，创世史诗有《查姆》《阿细的先基》《梅葛》《阿黑西尼摩》《尼苏夺节》等，译文文献长诗有《董永与七仙女》《凤凰记》《木荷与薇叶》《唐王游地府》《唐僧取经记》等。

云南彝族非纸质典籍最具代表性的是彝文摩崖。如昆明市禄劝彝族苗族自治县境内便有一通我国西南彝族地区历史较永久、留存较完整的长篇彝文金石铭刻——罗婺盛世史摩崖，刻面高206厘米×80厘米，镌刻于明嘉靖十年（1531年），迄今已有480多年，记述了武定凤氏土司14代350多年间的兴盛史。

云南每一个少数民族都拥有或者曾经拥有过或多或少的非纸质典籍。新中国成立以后特别是20世纪80年代后，很多的非纸质典籍得到了抢救保护，有的收藏于各级各类收藏机构，有的陈列于各类博物馆，有的已有了相关的整理研究成果。但更多的非纸质典籍，如深藏山野的摩崖石刻正经历着风吹日晒、沧海桑田，有的还曾经历过灭顶之灾；如壮族骨刻散布民间、无人释读，研究者有意寻访亦难见其真颜；又如纳西族木牌因仪式物品使用禁忌、用完即毁，难寻旧物……如此种种不止是云南少数民族非纸质典籍面临的生境，也是少数民族古籍所面临的困境。

三

文化是民族的根脉，是人类的精神家园，是一个民族凝聚力、生命力、创造力的源泉，是国家强盛的重要支撑。少数民族古籍真实而生动地记录了少数民族的历史发展进程，蕴含着少数民族特有的精神价值、思维方式和非凡的想象力、创造力，是人类文明的瑰宝，是中国珍贵的文化遗产。在长期的传播交流过程中，少数民族古籍发挥着积极进取的价值取向和经世致用的社会功能。一部优秀的民族古籍作品，其在民族社会中的价值远远超出了一个学科的专业范畴，代表了一个民族在某个专业领域的认知、反映了一个民族的某个历史发展阶段，甚或承载、再现了一个民族的社会事实和历史走向。加强少数民族古籍抢救和保护，对于丰富中华文化宝库，全面了解中华民族的发展历程，构建平等团结互助和谐的社会主义新型民族关系，推动民族团结进步事业，具有重要的历史意义和现实意义。

中华人民共和国成立后，在各级党委、政府的领导下，经过几代古籍工作者筚路蓝缕的努力，云南省少数民族古籍抢救保护和翻译整理出版工作取得了显著成绩。本着“抢救为主，保护第一”的原则，抢救了少数民族文字文献古籍3万余册（卷），口传古籍1万余种，以《纳西东巴古籍译注全集》《中国贝叶经全集》《彝族毕摩经典译注全集》《云南少数民族古籍珍本集成》《红河彝族文化遗产古籍典藏》《云南少数民族古典史诗全集》《云南少数民族叙事长诗全集》等为代表的民族古籍抢救保护成果引起国内外的广泛关注。但是，于卷帙浩繁的少数民族古籍而言，目前的抢救保护、翻译整理成果不过是沧海一粟。初略估算，除已征集保管的少数民族古籍以外，云南仍有7万余册（卷）的少数民族文字文献古籍散存民间。由于保管不善或无人传承等诸多原因，许多散存民间的古籍难于做到活态传承，佚失、损毁现象严重，抢救保护迫在眉睫。就云南少数民族非纸质典籍而言，其生境尤令人担忧。部分可移动的、具有文物价值的非纸质古籍，多数已被各级各类机构、企业、私人征集收藏，这样的抢救保护最大化地彰显了此类古籍的文物价值，但这些民族古籍收而藏之后，原本在民间尚能活态传承的民族智慧结晶极易成为待在深闺无人识的宝贝；少量仍存于民间的，亦不乏寻访之人，各色寻访者在山乡村寨走访寻宝，有的甚至被倒卖流到境外。而诸多不可以移动的非纸质古籍的生境更是让人心生惋惜，这些承载着民族文化的石刻、摩崖多隐匿深山，常年经受着日晒雨淋以致文字符号或字迹模糊、难于辨识，或直接被人为损毁。石刻、摩崖受自然侵蚀逐渐消失，这是事物发展的自然规律，但对于民族文化而言是一个让人痛心的巨大损失。

我们在做这套丛书的过程中，也亲历和见证了数次痛心的时刻。2011年起，在云南省财政厅、云南省民族宗教事务委员会的支持下，我们一直在持续开展“云南省百项少数民族文化精品工程”项目《云南少数民族古籍珍本集成》。同时，按照《国家民委关于印发全国少数民族古籍保护工作“十三五”规划通知》的要求，“基本完成全国少数民族古籍普查工作。会同相关部门全力推进普查工作，摸清各地少数民族古籍资源。建立健全普查登记管理制度，构建普查登记平台，对各地少数民族古籍普查情况进行录入、统计、汇总，形成全国少数民族古籍普查登记目录档案”。本着“摸家底、建平台”的目的，我们在云南全省范围内开展了少数民族古籍普查、采录工作。为此，我们访遍云南各州市的少数民族古籍收藏机构，走访古籍传承人、收藏爱好者，足迹几遍及云南全省。2016年，我们在迪庆藏族自治州调研时，迪庆藏族自治州藏学研究院的同志为我们介绍了州内非纸质典籍的留存分布情况，提到在维西傈僳族自治县塔城镇附近一个山坡上有很多藏文石刻。我们在电脑里看到了该院数年前实地调研时拍摄的照片，从中可以看到半面山坡都是石刻，都是一些有些年代的文化遗存。我们异常兴奋，因为这个石刻分布地和发现唐代藏文碑刻《格子碑》的格子村相距仅数里，又隐匿深山，难保不是一些有价值的非纸质典籍。遗憾的是，因此行我们未携带拍摄设备，心想留待日后再专程前来调研。未想此次擦肩而过，却错失了一睹其风采的机会。2018 年 5 月，我们组织了专业的拍摄、传拓人员前往迪庆州，一行人在迪庆州藏学院相关同志的带领下，经历修路堵车、徒步山林，风尘仆仆地来到那片山坡。可眼前的景象却让我们傻眼了，哪里还见得到石刻，只见坡头有一道高五六米的混着石头的土堆，下方红土里稀稀拉拉种了一些重楼。几经周折联系上村委会的同志，方得知该村为发展农业经济，特地请了推土机来平整了土地，这些石刻已经被埋到了土堆下。这只是我们在开展云南少数民族古籍抢救保护工作中经历的几乎不值一提的一件小事，这样的事情不止在迪庆，在全省各地都在发生着；不止石刻、摩崖，纸质文献、丝帛素书、竹木简牍无不面临着这样的生存困境。倾心于民族文化抢救保护的人们深感痛心疾首，却也深深地感受到，仅凭一个部门、一些群体去抢救保护，确实是势单力薄。基于这样的现状，抢救保护非纸质典籍确实是迫在眉睫。基于经费、人员、技术等各方面的制约，哪怕是采用最简单、最传统的办法，先把这些文化遗存的影像留下来，供社会科学研究使用，同时呼吁全社会共同关注民族古籍的抢救保护，这是一件意义深远的事情，也是本丛书策划之初最真实的出发点。

长期以来，云南人民出版社对云南少数民族古籍的抢救保护、整理出版工作给予了极大的支持。2016 年，将云南少数民族非纸质典籍抢救保护项目申报国家民族文字图书出版资金资助。云南省少数民族古籍整理出版规划办公室于数年前就多次到民族地区征集典籍，了解线索，拍摄图片。经过数年的努力，由丽江市博物院、丽江东巴文化研究院、丽江市玉龙纳西族自治县图书馆等单位和一些民间收藏爱好者收藏的云南非纸质典籍最终得以在此书中整合出版。为收集这些非纸质典籍，相关人员付出了辛勤劳动，足迹几遍及云南全省。大量的原数据采集回来后，我们在典籍的分类整合上却遇到了前所未有的困难。云南各少数民族的非纸质典籍载体可谓琳琅满目，每种载体类型古籍的数量和质量参差不齐，作为丛书汇总出版既要全面涵盖具有代表性的非纸质典籍的载体类型，又要兼顾覆盖各民族的非纸质典籍；既要鉴别甄选各民族非纸质典籍的珍品、精品，又要尽可能地考虑民族古籍在民族社会中的情感价值；既要客观地收录古籍珍品，又要考虑每卷图书的体量和规模。几经求证，严格按照民族古籍学的学科分类对云南的非纸质典籍进行归类，几乎是不可能的。我们只能对倾尽全力收集到的非纸质典籍做个大概的分类，各卷再细分类目。少数民族古籍的抢救保护是一项长期的工作，不是朝夕之功。我们想全面呈现云南非纸质典籍的精品、珍品，在实际工作中会不断发现新典籍、扩充新的类目，所以丛书难免有不当之处，唯有祈求方家海涵、指正。

总的说来，本丛书是云南少数民族非纸质典籍的第一次集成和汇总。它将以往秘不外传的众多少数民族古籍珍品第一次集中展示于世人面前，不论学术价值、史料价值，还是传世、鉴赏、收藏价值等都具有诸多独特性，在保护各民族文化遗产、弘扬各民族优秀文化、增进民族团结、促进中华民族共有精神家园建设等方面具有重要意义。

General Introduction

China is a unified multi-ethnic country. Various ethnic minorities have created and accumulated rich and colorful historic culture, while leaving a vast number of ancient books and records in the process of long-term historical development. Recording social process, historical trends and cultural connotations from different perspectives and reflecting wisdom, civilization achievements and the essence style from various sides, these ancient books and records are an important part of Chinese culture, a unique carrier for cultural inheritance, and a real reflection of the diversified but integrated historical pattern in China. Ancient books and records of ethnic minorities are an indispensable and unique part. Yunnan has long been enjoying the good reputation as "Museum of Ethnic Culture". Ancestors of ethnic minorities have created voluminous written documents and countless oral literature. A great diversity of language record types are involved in the ancient books of ethnic minorities. The contents of the records are extensive and profound, and the carrier forms are more complicated. Besides, there are inscriptions recording the historical events such as the official vows, merits and achievements, virtues of ancient wise men, awarding and imperial mandate appointments. Moreover, there are cliff engravings carved on the cliffs to depict the production and living situations as well as the cognitions of the ancestors. There are also sutras and scriptures carved in stone, stone-carved statues of gods, and Pattra-leaf Scriptures carved on pattra leaves with the stencil pen (a cutting tool used in carving seals, etc.). These are the non-paper ancient books and records of ethnic minorities to be collected and recorded in this series of book.

I

Ancient books and records of ethnic minorities in China (hereinafter referred to as ancient books and records of ethnic minorities) refer to ancient books and records, inscriptions, oral inheritance materials and other documents of 55 ethnic minorities in their respective languages in history, contents of which cover politics, philosophy, history, religion, military affairs, literature, art, languages, geography, the celestial almanac, economy, medicine and other fields. 1911 is generally taken as the lower limit for the time category of ancient books and records of ethnic minorities. However, due to historical characteristics of various ethnic minorities and differences in the existence of the ancient books and records, some of them may be extended to 1949 in accordance with the actual situation of ancient books of various ethnic minorities.

Ancient books and records of ethnic minorities are an important part of Chinese traditional culture as well as an important study subject of ancient books, records and literature. In the past, there were no comprehensive or systematic explanations on such subject in the traditional research. Nevertheless, with the establishment of various levels and kinds of departments on ancient books of ethnic minorities in the 1980s, work of ancient books and records of ethnic minorities ushered in the spring. In 1981, the Central Committee of the Communist Party of China pointed out in *The Instructions on Sorting-out of Ancient Chinese Books* that "it is a fundamental task that affects later generations to sort out ancient books and records and inherit the precious cultural heritage of the nation." The State Council, in forwarding the notification of *The Request from the State Civil Affairs Commission on the Rescue and Sorting-out of Ancient Books and Records of Ethnic Minorities*, stressed that "ancient books and records of ethnic minorities are part of the precious cultural heritage of the nation, and it is a fundamental task to rescue and to sort-out them" in 1984. In accordance with the instructions, corresponding departments responsible for the work of ancient books and records of ethnic minorities were set up at the national and local levels to carry out the rescue, protection, sorting-out and publication of ancient books of ethnic minorities. Over the three decades past, relevant personnel responsible for ancient books and records of ethnic minorities have been taking the mission of "rescuing books, people and disciplines" as their mission, and achieved fruitful goals. However, this task is also faced with numerous difficulties, and it is extremely difficult to push it forward. With the rapid development of society, depletion of ancient book and record resources and the outflow of talents for ancient books and records of ethnic minorities become increasingly severe. Besides, the development of the discipline on ancient books and records of ethnic minorities is relatively backward, and the basic theoretical research is very weak. For instance, there are so many voluminous ancient books and records of ethnic minorities in China that the classification of such books is still inconclusive. Moreover, the definition of "ethnic ancient books and records" is a very important issue, but relevant opinions are divergent. [1] Here, we have no intention to make systematical sorting, but just to clarify the inclusion scope of non-paper ancient books and records of ethnic minorities.

During the rescue, protection, sorting-out and publication of ancient books and records of ethnic minorities, especially since 1997, when sorting out ancient books and records of ethnic minorities conducted throughout the country on *Summary of the Catalog of Ancient Books and Records of Chinese Ethnic Minorities,* we habitually divide ethnic ancient books and records into two categories: literal and non-literal categories. Ethnic ancient books and records of literal category can be divided into the following three subcategories: first, historical documents, books and records recorded in the current and ancient languages of ethnic minorities. Secondly, ancient literature, books and records relevant to the ethnic minorities recorded in Chinese. Thirdly, inscriptions related to the ethnic minorities recorded in the Chinese and minority languages. Ethnic ancient books and records of non-literal category mainly refer to various kinds of historical and cultural documents handed down orally by the ethnic minorities in history. [2] In view of the different carrier forms, ancient books and records of ethnic minorities were further divided into four categories of books, inscriptions, documents as well as lectures and songs in the implementation of *Summary of the Catalog of Ancient Books and Records of Ethnic Minorities in China.* [3] Among them, the classical binding forms of books and records of ethnic minorities in history are comprehensively included in the category of books; stone-tablet and cliff carvings, epigraphs, inscriptions carved on the sacrificial utensil, the elegy volume, and bamboo and wooden engravings are included in the category of inscriptions. Various kinds of notices, contracts, leaflets, letters of notifications, correspondence, bills, duplicates,

① In the preface of *Investigation and Research on Ancient Books and Records of Ethnic Minorities in Yunnan* (The Ethnic Publishing House, Edition 2010), Li Guowen made a systematic review of the understanding and definition of "ancient books and records of ethnic minorities" in the academic circle. In recent years, there have been some discussions on the relevant research, but the views have nothing to brag about.

② The Research Office of Ancient Books and Records of Ethnic Minorities for National Ethnic Affairs Commission: "Preface" of *Volume of the Naxi Ethnic Group for Summary of Catalogue of Ancient Books and Records of Ethnic Minorities in China,* Edition 2003 by Encyclopedia of China Publishing House.

③ The Research Office of Ancient Books and Records of Ethnic Minorities for National Ethnic Affairs Commission: "Preface" of *Volume of the Hani Ethnic Group for Summary of Catalogue of Ancient Books and Records of Ethnic Minorities in China,* Page 10 of Edition 2008 by Encyclopedia of China Publishing House.

conventions, regulations, licenses, archives, letters, notes and other documents are included in the documentary category of ethnic ancient books and records. The myths, legends, stories and ballads with historical and cultural value related to ethnic origin, migration of ethnic minorities and the origin of civilization and other oral inheritance of ethnic minorities are included in the category of lectures and songs. According to the four-classification method of the literature carriers of ancient books and records of ethnic minorities, the compilation of various ethnic volumes in *Summary of the Catalog of Ancient Books and Records of Ethnic Minorities in China* is in line with the objective reality and effective. Meanwhile, the classification method has great influence because of the wide scope and long duration of the task. Nevertheless, since ethnic ancient books and records are classified according to the carrier forms, whether books and records of "documentary category" can be taken as an individual category is still to be considered. What is the "literature carrier"? Explanations in five aspects have been provided for the word "carrier", one of which refers to "the material form carrying knowledge or information". As the name suggests, "literature carrier" is the material carrier of literature. Materials such as paper, silk, cloth, wood, leaves, animal bones, stones, stone implements, and animal skins can be used as literature carriers. The word "document" can be dated far back in time, which could be seen in the historical records as early as in the Han and Jin Dynasties. Besides, it referred to a type of written documents taking the written language as the main method to record information, which could be divided into official and private documents, various kinds of notifications, contracts, leaflets, letter of notification, correspondence, bills, duplicates, conventions, regulations, licenses, archives, letters, notes and other documents by nature. Seen from this aspect, a document is a concept defined by the content of literature. In the ancient books and records of ethnic minorities in Yunnan, there are different forms of material carriers, such as documents written on paper or carved or chiseled on bricks and stones.

Furthermore, the concept and classification of ethnic ancient books and records mentioned in *Ethnic Ancient Books and Records* by Mr. Wu Gu were quite representative. He believed that "ethnic ancient books and records refer to all the cultural carriers of ethnic minorities who once lived or are living within the territory of the People's Republic of China, which are recorded in words, symbols with certain cultural meanings (prototypes of written language), and in oral languages carried over in history. This kind of cultural carriers can be divided into four major categories, i.e., ancient books and records of original, inscriptions, oral inheritance materials and written carriers." ①According to the classification by Mr. Wu Gu, various kinds of historical documents passed on by the ethnic minorities in history with bamboo slips, cloth and paper as the carriers, including books, archives, documents, imperial edicts, household registrations, contracts, ultimatums, letters, notifications, township rules and folk contracts written in various ethnic languages, are classified as ancient books and records with written carriers. In the numerous classification methods, the category of inscriptions (or known as ancient books and records with ancient bronzes and stone tablet carriers) and the category of lectures and songs (or called as oral inheritance materials ancient books and records) can be regarded as separate categories according to the carrier form without many controversies. However, due to different names, the connotations and extensions of "inscriptions and ancient books and records with ancient bronze and stone tablet carriers" vary significantly. Inscriptions cover a broader and more comprehensive range of material carriers and are not restricted to stone implements, including stone, bamboo, wooden and bone carvings and cliff engravings, implements and other materials. In essence, the category of inscriptions covers part of the original carriers of ancient books and records as defined by Mr. Wu Gu. However, "inscriptions" emphasizes the writing modes of ancient books rather than the carrier forms. The category of "ancient books and records with carriers of ancient bronzes and stone tablets" is narrowly defined, which does not include such carrier forms as bone and bamboo carvings. Although Mr. Wu Gu further defined the category of "original carrier", "it referred to material objects or symbols provided with a certain special meaning and used to record events or express meanings at the beginning of formation of the written language of an ethnic minority...Each ethnic minority has left over a large number of vivid and detailed original ancient books and records relevant to record keeping of events through wooden carving, knot tying and record keeping with material objects." ② Seen from this concept, it is obviously improper to classify bone, bamboo and wooden carvings into the ancient books and records with original carriers.

In conclusion, due to the different environments and historical development process of ethnic minorities in China, the carrier forms of ancient books and records of ethnic minorities are diverse. Some are rare but extremely precious, while some have disappeared in history. It is extremely difficult to classify the numerous ancient books and records of ethnic minorities in China with one or several carrier forms. Besides, it is hard to make comprehensive

① Wu Gu: *Studies on Ethnic Ancient Books and Records*, Edition 1994 by Yunnan Ethnic Publishing House, P6 .

② Wu Gu: *Studies on Ethnic Ancient Books and Records*, Edition 1994 by Yunnan Ethnic Publishing House, P10 .

generalizations. We choose the "non-paper" carrier forms as the point of penetration. In addition to paper carriers, ancient books and records with tangible physical carriers of ethnic minorities in Yunnan are all the objects to be included by us, for the purpose of compiling and publishing the ancient books with non-paper carriers of various ethnic minorities in Yunnan, which are scattered in libraries, museums, archive centers and other collection institutions in various regions, as well as the scattered folk collections, which have not been made public for a long time and have significant historical and cultural value, as well as value of cultural relics and scientific research.

II

Yunnan is a province where multiple ethnic minorities live in compact communities. 25 ethnic minorities with a population of more than 5,000 people have been living there for generations. Chinese is generally used in the three ethnic minorities (the Hui Ethnic minority, the Shui Ethnic minority and Manchu). However, the other 22 ethnic minorities use 26 languages (some ethnic minorities even use two or more languages). Among them, 14 ethnic minorities have 23 kinds of writing or spelling systems, and some of them use two or more written languages. Moreover, they have left over voluminous ethnic ancient books and records. According to the statistics, there are more than 100,000 books (volumes) of ancient books and records scattered in Yunnan, including those in Tibetan, Naxi Dongba, Yi, Zhuang characters, Lisu and Bai characters, Hangui characters in the Pumi Ethnic Minority, and Dai and Yao characters. As for other ethnic minorities such as the Hani, the Miao, he Lahu, the Wa, the Jingpo, the Bulang, the Buyi, the Achang, the Nu, the Jinuo, the De'ang, the Shui and the Dulong Ethnic Minorities, although they don't have their own ancient languages, they pass on their historic culture orally, with rich and colorful oral documents. Moreover, there are tens of thousands of creation epics, migration epics, narrative poems, myths, legends, sacrifice songs, labor songs, living custom songs, etc. Furthermore, there are still a large number of oral literatures passed down among the ethnic minorities with ancient languages. There are over 40,000 kinds of oral ancient records passed on in the ethnic minorities Yunnan, covering politics, philosophy, law, history, religion, military affairs, literature, art, language, writing, geography, astronomy, calendar, economy, medicine and other fields.

The ancient books and records of ethnic minorities in Yunnan have been provided with the characteristics of huge reserves, long history and various carriers, among which there are lots of non-paper ancient books and records. All the ethnic minorities once experienced or are experiencing a period of history without written languages. In order to facilitate communication and convey meanings, some "material languages" or "symbol languages" that can be used to record events and convey meanings were created, for instance, the original cultural carriers such as record-keeping through knots tying, wood carving and with leaf letters. Under the special cultural circumstances, these original cultural carriers were provided with different symbolic meanings. With the development of human society, especially after the creation of the written languages, the practical value of the original cultural carriers in the groups is gradually diluted, and some even disappeared in history. However, the practical value of these original cultural carriers has far exceeded their cultural and historical-relic value. Whether the original cultural carriers can be included into the category of ethnic ancient books and records is still controversial. In view of the fact that the number of original cultural carriers retained in various ethnic minorities in Yunnan is limited, the majority of the carriers were discovered recently, and that it is difficult to distinguish their ethnic minority classification and make interpretations, they are not included in this book. Based on the different natural environment in the distribution areas of various ethnic minorities, the distinctive historical development process, and the unique traditional culture, it can be said that there are a wide variety of the carriers for the over 100,000 discovered ancient books and records of ethnic minorities in Yunnan. Cloths, bamboos, animal bones and skins, ancient bronzes and stone tablet implements and other materials have become the carriers of ancient books and records of various ethnic minorities in different historical periods. Here, we generally introduce the ancient books and records of several ethnic minorities with a large number of non-paper ancient books and records as well as the representative carriers.

1. Ancient Books and Records of the Naxi Ethnic Minority

Currently, there are more than 1,000 kinds (over 30,000 volumes) of Dongba ancient books and records collected at home and abroad (books of roughly the same contents are taken as one kind), commonly known as "Dongba Scriptures". Besides, most are pictorial hieroglyphic-writing transcripts; some are mixed with pictorial pictographs and Geba scripts; a very few are pure Geba scripts. There are mainly ancient religious books and records, and documents and inscriptions in Dongba characters, and oral documents passed down from mouth to mouth by the Naxi Ethnic Minority are also included. Contents of the Dongba ancient books and records cover social history, language, philosophy, religion, customs, literature and art, astronomy, medicine and other fields, which can be regarded as "the encyclopedia of the ancient Naxi Ethnic

Minority". According to the contents, the ancient books and records can be divided into the category of praying for prolonged life including *The Return of Remote Ancestors, Animal Sacrifice, Battle between the Great Roc and the Shu Synopsis*, the category of ghosts and disaster elimination such as *Luban Lurao, The War between the "Dong" and "Su"Tribes, The Creation, White Bat's Collection of Scriptures*, the category of the release of the souls from suffering in the funerals such as *Killing the Devil Ghost and Helpful Ghost, Gao Lequ Recall of Father's Soul, The Origin of Human Migration*, and *The Origin of Horses*, the category of divination such as *The Book of the Divination of the Earth, Divination with Hatem Bagato*, and *The Skills of Divination by Interpreting Dreams*, and the category concerning dance, medicine and folk songs such as *Dongba Dance Notation, The Book of Medicine*, and *the Model of Folk Songs*, as well as the Ruanke Dongba Scripture with unique regional features at Youmi Village in Ninglang County of Lijiang City.

Among the Naxi non-paper ancient books and records, the most representative, the most widely used and the most abundant ones are the wooden-plaque paintings on wooden plaques and the scroll paintings on cloth. As a kind of primitive painting art with a long history, the wooden-plaque paintings is a work of Dongba art in its infancy stage, which is mostly used in large-scale sacrificial activities. Generally, the wooden plaques are approximately 60 cm in length, 10 cm in width and 1 cm in thickness, and the contents are in accordance with the records of Dongba picture copybooks. According to the sacrificial functions, they can be divided into god and ghost plaques, door plates, debt-collecting, cursing and other plaques. The picture is peculiar in shape, simple in appearance, straightforward in line, and bold, natural and fluent in brushwork, which is provided with the primitive art characteristics of the ancestors. Scroll paintings, known as "Pulaozhang" in Naxi Language, are statues of gods painted on homespun cloth by Dongba people with mineral pigments, and are all works tending to be sophisticated when the Dongba paintings have entered a developed stage, including multiple types such as long scrolls, multiple and single pieces. A great god or guardian god is mainly depicted in each scroll painting representing a certain god and the divine circle where it lived. The painting is used in Dongba religious rituals and directly hung above the altar. Different statues of gods are hung in different ceremonies. Representative scroll paintings include statues of Dingbasheluo (founder of the Dongba Religion), Yiguwoge (great god of the Dongba Religion), Youma (god of wars), God Dong (god of Yang), God Shu (god of Yin), Sayiweide and Road Maps of Gods. Among them, the painting of the road to heaven are the most original and representative masterpiece in Dongba scroll paintings, with a width of 16~30 cm and a length of approximately 15 meters. Three parts of the hell,the world of mortals and the heaven are successively depicted on the scroll paintings, with more than 360 individuals, gods, ghosts and over 70 kinds of odd birds and monsters. It is known as the longest straight scroll in the history of the Chinese art, and enjoys the reputation of "the first long scroll of the ancient religious painting", which is provided with high cultural and artistic research value. The contents, nature and use of road maps of gods are basically consistent. However, due to different carrier materials, pigments and painting techniques, each the painting of the road to heaven has its unique artistic style.

2. Ancient Books and Records of the Zhuang Ethnic Minority

The Zhuang Ethnic Minority has its own language and characters, and Zhuang Language is a category of the Zhuang-Dai language branch of the Zhuang-Dong Group of Sino-Tibetan Languages, divided into two big dialects of the north and south. Zhuang Language was already in the embryonic stage in the Pre-Qin Period. In the Sui and Tang Dynasties, ancestors of the Zhuang Ethnic Minority recorded Zhuang Language with Chinese characters, and invented the square Zhuang characters, called as "Tuzi"or "Tusuzi". Besides, they used ancient Zhuang characters to record folk stories, and record scriptures, genealogy, inscriptions, accounting, etc. Besides, a batch of ancient books in square Zhuang characters has been handed down. Ancient Zhuang books and records are known as "Shimo", "Shiduozai", "Shiya", etc. in Zhuang Language. "Shi" in Zhuang Language refers to "books", which are mainly transcribed on the gauze paper made of barks of the Shapi trees, written on the Zheka paper made from fresh bamboos or tapa. The ancient books of the Zhuang Ethnic Minority are in a wide variety and a large number, including books recording the rites, scriptures and doctrines of the Mo Religion such as *Buluotuo Lection*, *Mohetai*, *Maxian*, and *De Dai Shan Deng E*, narrative poems and ancient songs reflecting simplicity world view and values such as *Pangu Song*, *Bubo*, and *Mozedu*, folk seven-character narrative poems such as *Maohong*, *Dongyong* and *Shun'er*. Moreover, there are also quite a few *Jibu Scriptures* representing art of painting as well as the religious painting "Laimo", contents of which cover history, language, literature, art, philosophy, religion, astronomy, calendar and many other fields and can be said to be extensive and profound and gorgeous.

The non-paper ancient books and records of the Zhuang Ethnic Minority are represented by cliff engravings, bone carvings and drawing books and records. The first category is cliff engravings. There are hundreds of cliff engravings in the current distribution area of the Zhuang Ethnic Minority. According to the existing archaeological data, there are many original carved and painted art relics in the distribution area of today's Zhuang Ethnic Minority. Although it is difficult to clearly define the ethnic group of these archaeological relics, it is certain that the ancestors of the Zhuang Ethnic Minority are the creators and owners of these paintings. The most representative cliff engravings are distributed in the Zhuang and Miao Autonomous Prefecture of Wenshan. There are 11 places (12 locations), including the cliff engravings on the Dawang Cliff in the Malipo, Heiqinglong in Qiubei, Kazi in the Yanshan, Nongka in Guangnan and the Shizi Mountain in Benggu of Xichou, covering an area of approximately 5,430 square meters, with more than 170 engravings and over 400 designs. The second type is bone-carved books. The ancestors of the Zhuang Ethnic Minority in Yunnan had a long history of carving patterns on utensils, animal bones and even human body, which are still passed on and used in some areas. Among them, the most famous one is bone-carved almanac calculator in the Zhuang Ethnic Minority. The Committee of Ethnic and Religious Affairs of Zhuang and Miao Autonomous Prefecture of Wenshan discovered 58 bone carvings within its territory. Bone carvings, known as "Jiabake" and "Wajiaba" in Zhuang Language, refer to graphic symbols and books engraved on the bone pieces, which were the utensils used by the primitive people for calculating calendars and divination. Animal bones were usually engraved with figures, tables, coffins, plants, bows and arrows, animals, dry railings, sun patterns and other images, which are pictographs with both aesthetic and memory functions. The third type refers to the statues of gods. Majority of the engravings in the Zhuang Ethnic Minority are statues of gods, with diverse types and abundant works, implying the secular concept of avoiding evil by the power of "god". The aesthetic attitude and emotion are intertwined. According to its content, shapes and use, it can be roughly divided into three categories: long-scroll statues of gods in the Mo Religion, religious wall pictures and divination paintings. Among them, long-scroll statues of gods in the Mo Religion are among the unique religious images of the religion, which is inherited and used by the priests in the Mo Religion. Painted on the homespun linen, the statues are in long vertical-scroll form. Besides, column painting are made, mostly used for funeral and tomb-sweeping ceremonies.

3. Ancient Books of the Dai Ethnic Minority

The Dai Ethnic Minority has its own ethnic written language. Most of the ancient books and records in the Dai Language are carving and writing copies, manuscripts and transcripts. There are two kinds of ancient books and records, i.e., pattra-leaf and paper (tissue and vellum paper) books. The shape and structure are generally composed of the form of two plaques sandwiched together, folding and traditional thread binding, which are mainly spread in the Dai areas of Xishuangbanna, Dehong, Baoshan, Pu 'er, Lincang, Honghe and other prefectures and cities.

According to the contents, ancient books of Dai Language can be divided into the religious category such as *Lang Si She Bu Xian Zai, Prayer for Chicken Sacrifice to the Water God, Prayer for the Soul of the Rice Sacrifice*, and *The Conjuring Words*, the political and historical category such as *The Le History* and *Xuanfu History of Menglian*, the literature and art category including *Batamaga Pengshangluo, Lan Ga Xi He*, and *Li Feng*, as well as the categories of astronomy and calendar, farmland water conservancy, medicine, theory monograph, military martial arts, language and characters, translation and other categories.

Non-paper ancient book carriers of the Dai Ethnic Minority are provided with the characteristics of a variety of forms and large quantities, the most representative of which are the silverware, pattra-leaf scriptures and ancient painting books of the Dai Ethnic Minority. Among them, pattra-leaf scriptures are the most typical non-paper ancient books and records. The pattra-leaf scriptures, known as "Tanlan" in Dai Language, are carved on specially-made pattra leaves with the stencil pen (a cutting tool used in carving seals, etc.) by local people. Furthermore, wall and cloth paintings and other non-paper painting books and records are also quite distinctive.

4. Ancient Books of the Yi Ethnic Minority

The Yi Ethnic Minority has its own language and writing system. Yi Language is a category of the Yi language branch of the Tibeto-Burman Group of Sino-Tibetan Languages, divided into six big dialects of the east, west, south, north, central and southeast regions. The Yi Ethnic Minority has its own ancient writing system, which was called "Yi Scriptures" "Cuan characters", "Luoluo characters", etc. in ancient Chinese books and records. Currently, they are collectively known as "ancient Yi Language". Each character pattern represents a literal meaning, and there are various ways of writing. There are over 10,000 character forms in the existing ancient Yi character, with over 1,000 words in common use. In history, ancestors of the Yi Ethnic Minority used ancient Yi Language to write voluminous literature and books as well as numerous inscriptions, covering politics, military affairs, philosophy, religion, history, geography, language, writing system, literature, art, astronomy, calendar, medicine, health and other fields. The ancient Yi books and records popular in the Yi Ethnic Minority in modern times mainly include paper, leather, cloth, bone, cliff, wooden slips, wood engraving, inscriptions, seals and other carrier forms, of which, paper books account for an absolute proportion, including transcripts and wood-carving printed copies. There are over 20,000 volumes (pieces) of ancient books and records in Yi Language in existence, a majority of which are transcripts and minority are wood-carving printed copies. There are over 20,000 volumes (pieces) of ancient books and records in Yi Language in existence. Ancient Books and records in Yi Language in Yunnan can be divided into ancient books and records in Yi Language in South Yunnan, Luquan and Wuding, Sani, Azhe, Xuanwei, Luoping and the north. The more representative books include the traditional religious ritual ancient books such as *Wucha, Mencha, The Scripture for Guiding passage,* The *Scripture for Dragon Worship, The Scripture for Prayer to the Heaven for Rain, Lu Zi Nan Dao, Nao Si Gu, The Scripture for Recalling the Soul of the Dead,* and *Ni Bu Mu Si,* the famous literary work such as *Ashima* and *Nimi Poem,* the creation epics such as *Chamu, Axi's xianji, Meige, Ahei Xinimo,* and *Ni Su Duo Jie,* and the literature long poems in translation such as *Dong Yong and Qi Xiannü Celestial, The Phoenix, Muhe and Weiye , Tangwang's Wandering to the Other World,* and *Tang Monks' Journey for Buddhist Scriptures.*

The most representative non-paper ancient books and records of the Yi Ethnic Minority in Yunnan are cliff engravings in Yi Language. For instance, the Cliff Engraving Depicting History of the Flourishing Age of Luowu (the carved area is 206cm×80cm in height) is the long-piece inscription in Yi Language with a relatively large history and retained relatively complete in the Yi Ethnic Minority in the southwest region of China within the territory of Yi and Miao Autonomous County in Luquan of Kunming City, which was engraved in the 10th year during the reign of Emperor Jiajing of the Ming Dynasty (1531A. D.). It has a history of over 480 years, recording the prosperous history of 14 generations of Feng's hereditary headmen in Wuding in more than 350 years.

Each ethnic minority in Yunnan has or once had more or less non-paper ancient books and records. Since the establishment of the People's Republic of China, especially in the 1980s, many non-paper ancient books and records have been rescued and protected. Some are preserved in various collection institutions at all levels, some are displayed in various kinds of museums, and some have received relevant research results. Nevertheless, a great many non-paper ancient books and records, such as cliff engravings hidden in the deep mountains are exposed to the weather, have been changed a lot, or even have disappeared. For instance, bone carvings in the Zhuang Ethnic Minority were scattered here and there, and no one has interpreted them. The investigators intended to seek and discover the profound mysteries, but they failed. For another example, due to the taboo of using ritual items, wooden plaques were destroyed immediately after use, it is difficult to find the ancestors' utensils... All these are not only the existing situation faced by the non-paper books and records of ethnic minorities in Yunnan, but also the dilemma faced by the ancient records of ethnic minorities.

III

Culture is the root of the ethnic groups, the spiritual home of mankind, the source of a nation's cohesion, vitality and creativity, and an important support for a strong and prosperous country. The ancient books and records of ethnic minorities are true and vivid records of the historical development process of ethnic minorities, which contain the unique spiritual values, ways of thinking and extraordinary imagination and creativity of ethnic minorities. They are the treasures of human civilization and the precious cultural heritage of China. Ancient books and records of ethnic minorities have been playing an active value orientation role and a social function of practical application in the long process of spreading and communication. The value of an excellent work of ethnic ancient books and records in the national society goes far beyond the professional scope of a discipline, representing the cognition of a nation in a certain professional field, reflecting a certain historical development stage of a nation, or even bearing and representing the social facts and historical trend of a nation. It is important historical and practical significance to strengthen the rescue and protection of ancient books and records of ethnic minorities for enriching the treasure house of Chinese culture, comprehensively understanding the development course of the Chinese nation, building a new socialist ethnic relationship of equality, solidarity, mutual assistance and harmony, and promoting the cause of ethnic unity and progress.

After the establishment of the People's Republic of China, under the leadership of party committees and governments at all levels, remarkable achievements have been made in the rescue, protection, translation, collation and publication of ancient books and records of ethnic minorities in Yunnan Province through unremitting efforts of several generations of relevant working personnel on ancient books and records. Based on the principle of "rescue orientation, and protection first", more than 30,000 ancient books (volumes) of written literature and over 10,000 oral ancient records of ethnic minorities have been rescued. Moreover, *Complete Works of Translations and Annotations on Ancient Books and Records of Naxi Dongba*, *Complete Works of Chinese Pattra-leaf Scriptures*, *Integration of Rare Editions of Ancient Books and Records of Ethnic Minorities in Yunnan*, *Reservation of Ancient Books and Records of Cultural Heritage of the Yi Ethnic Minority in Honghe*, *Complete Works of Classical Epics of Ethnic Minorities in Yunnan*, *Complete Works of Narrative Poems of Ethnic Minorities in Yunnan* and other representative ethnic ancient book and record achievements have attracted extensive attentions at home and abroad. However, the current achievements of the rescue, protection, translation and compilation are not worth mentioning for the voluminous ancient books and records of ethnic minorities. It is roughly estimated that in addition to the collected and preserved ancient books and records of ethnic minorities, there are still more than 70,000 ancient books (volumes) of the ethnic minority literature scattered in Yunnan. Due to numerous reasons such as improper preservation or no inheritance, it is difficult to carry out active-state inheritance for many ancient books scattered among the people. Moreover, many ancient books are lost or damaged, so the rescue and protection task is urgent. The specific regional conditions of the non-paper ancient books and records of ethnic minorities in Yunnan are especially worrying. The majority of part of the movable, non-paper ancient books with cultural relic value have been collected and preserved by the institutions at all levels, enterprises and private people. The rescue and protection work maximizes the cultural value of such ancient books and records. However, after the collection and preservation of ancient books of ethnic minorities, the national wisdom crystallization, which could have been passed down in the folk in active state, can easily become the treasure in the private book cabinets that no one else knows. There are still various kinds of people paying visits to the mountains and villages to search for the small number of ancient books and records of ethnic minorities, some of which have been resold overseas at a profit. Meanwhile, the specific regional conditions for many immovable non-paper ancient books and records are even more regrettable. These stone carvings and cliff engravings bearing ethnic culture are mostly hidden in deep mountains, which are exposed to the weather all the year round. Therefore, the writing symbols or handwriting are so blurred that it is difficult to identify them, or they have directly been damaged by human beings. Natural erosion and gradual disappearance of the stone carvings and cliff engravings is the natural law of development, but it is a huge loss for the ethnic culture.

We have experienced and witnessed several painful moments during the preparation of this series of books. With the support of Yunnan Provincial Department of Finance and Yunnan Provincial Commission of Ethnic and Religious Affairs, we have been consistently pushing forward the project of *Integration of Rare Editions of Ancient Books and Records of Ethnic Minorities in Yunnan*, which is among the one hundred excellent cultural projects in Yunnan Province. Meanwhile, according to the requirements specified in *Notification on the 13th Five-year Plan for the Protection of Ancient Books and Records of Ethnic Minorities issued by National Ethnic Affairs Commission of the People's Republic of China*, "the national census on ancient books of ethnic minorities have been basically completed; the census work has been fully promoted together with relevant departments to find out the resources of ancient books and records of ethnic minorities in various regions. Moreover, the census registration management system shall be established and improved; and a census registration platform shall be constructed to enter, calculate and summarize the census information of ancient books and records of ethnic minorities in various regions, so that the national census registration catalogue of ancient books and records of ethnic minorities can be established." In line with the purpose of "understanding the basic condition and building a platform", we have conducted a general survey and collection of ancient books and records of ethnic minorities in Yunnan Province. For this purpose, we have visited the collection institutions of ancient books and records of ethnic minorities in every prefecture and city of Yunnan Province, and paid visits to the inheritors of ancient books and records and the collectors. Our footprints have almost covered all the regions of Yunnan Province. When we conducted research in Diqing Tibetan Autonomous Prefecture in 2016, the Research Institute of Tibetan Studies in Diqing Tibetan Autonomous Prefecture introduced the preservation and distribution of non-paper ancient books and records in the prefecture, and mentioned that there were many Tibetan stone carvings on the hillside near Tacheng Town of Weixi County. We found the pictures taken by the institute during the field research in the computer several years ago. We could see that half of the hillside was covered with stone carvings, which were all age-old cultural relics. We were so excited. Since there were only a few miles between the distribution location of the stone carvings and Gezi Village where the *Grid Tablet Inscription* engraved in Tibetan language in the Tang Dynasty, and the stone carvings were hidden in the deep mountain, there may be some valuable non-paper ancient records. Unfortunately, we didn't bring the shooting equipment with us, so we decided to go there for investigation later. We didn't expect that we had missed the chance to see its elegant style and features. In May 2018, we organized professional photo-taking, transferring and rubbing personnel to visit Diqing Tibetan Autonomous Prefecture. Led by relevant comrades of Tibetan Institute of Diqing Tibetan Autonomous Prefecture, the group went through the road repair, traffic jam, and hiking in the mountains and came to the hillside tirelessly. However, the scene shocked us, there was no stone carving at all, but a mound mixed with a stone of 5~6 meters in height on the slope. A few Paris polyphylla were planted in the red earth below. After several twists and turns, we got in touch with the comrades of the village committee, and learned that the village had specially assigned bulldozers to level the land so as to develop agricultural economy, and these stone carvings were buried under the mound. This is just a trivial matter we have experienced in the process of the rescue and protection of ancient books and records of ethnic minorities in Yunnan. Such things are happening not only in Diqing, but also in all the regions all over the province. All the stone carvings, cliff engraving, paper literature, silk books, bamboo-slip and wooden engraving are all confronted with such living dilemma. Personnel devoted to the rescue and protection of the ethnic culture felt deeply distressed, but deeply understand that the force of a department and even some groups is so weak to carry out the rescue and protection task. Based on such situation, it is urgent to rescue and protect non-paper ancient books and records. In view of the restriction of funds, personnel, technology and various other aspects, it is suggested that pictures of these culture heritages should be kept for the use of social science research even using the simplest and the most traditional way. Meanwhile, we call on the whole society to attach importance to the rescue and protection of ethnic ancient books and records, which is a profound cause, and also the most actual starting point at the beginning of planning of this series of books.

Yunnan People's Publishing House has offered vigorous supports to the rescue, protection, collation and publication of ancient books and records of ethnic minorities in Yunnan. The project of the rescue and protection of non-paper ancient books and records of ethnic minorities in Yunnan Province was funded by the publication fund for ancient books and records in the ethnic minority languages through application in 2016. Several years ago, Yunnan Provincial Planning Office of Sorting and Publishing Ancient Books of Ethnic Minorities collected ancient books and records from the ethnic minority areas for many times, trying to obtain the clues and take pictures. Yunnan non-paper ancient books and records collected by Lijiang Museum, Lijiang Dongba Culture Research Institute, the Library in Yulong Naxi Autonomous County of Lijiang and Yunnan non-paper ancient books and records collected by folk collectors are finally integrated and published in this book after years of efforts. In order to collect these non-paper ancient books and records, relevant personnel have made great efforts and their footprints almost covered the whole regions of Yunnan Province. After collecting a great deal of original data, we encountered unprecedented difficulties in the classification and integration of the ancient books and records. Carriers of the non-paper ancient books and records in various ethnic minorities can be said to be in a great variety, and the quantity and quality of each carrier type of ancient books and records are at different levels. Since it is taken as the carrier form of a series of books that are summarized and published and comprehensively cover the representative non-paper ancient books and records, it should also take the non-paper ancient books and records covering all the ethnic minorities into account. Not only shall the precious and fine works of non-paper ancient books and records of various ethnic minorities be identified and selected, but also the emotional value of ethnic ancient books in ethnic society shall be taken into consideration as much as possible. The precious ancient books shall be objectively collected and included, and the volume and scale of books shall be also taken into consideration. Through several confirmations, we find that it is almost impossible to classify the non-paper ancient books and records in Yunnan in accordance with the discipline classification of the ethnic ancient books and records. We can only make a general classification of the non-paper ancient books and records that we have collected with all our efforts, and then classify each volume into different subcategories. The rescue and protection of ancient books and records of ethnic minorities is a long-term painstaking task, which cannot be completed in a short period. We were expected to present the high-quality and precious works of Yunnan non-paper ancient books and records comprehensively, but we are constantly discovering new ancient books and records and expanding new categories in our practical work. Therefore, there are inevitably some improper aspects in the series of books, so we can only hope for the forgiveness and corrections of the experts earnestly.

In conclusion, this series of books are the first large-scale integration and collection of non-paper ancient books and records of ethnic minorities in Yunnan. It is for the first time that numerous ancient books and precious records of ethnic minorities, which have been kept secret in the past, are shown to the public. They have been provided with many unique features in terms of academic, historical, inheritance, appreciation and collection value. Moreover, it is of great significance in protecting the cultural heritage of various ethnic minorities, carrying forward their excellent culture, enhancing ethnic unity and promoting the construction of the common spiritual homeland of the Chinese Ethnic Peoples.

目录

云南少数民族非纸质典籍聚珍

YUNNAN SHAOSHU MINZU FEIZHIZHI DIANJI JUZHEN

纳西东巴卷轴画………… 001

卷轴挂画 ………………………… 007

神路图 ………………………… 104

神路图（一） ………………… 104
神路图（二） ………………… 134
神路图（三） ………………… 152
神路图（四） ………………… 182
神路图（五） ………………… 192

壮族神图长卷…………… 235

神图长卷（一） …………… 241
神图长卷（二） …………… 262
神图长卷（三） …………… 284
神图长卷（四） …………… 298
神图长卷（五） …………… 318

后记………………………… 335

YUNNAN SHAOSHU MINZU
FEIZHIZHI DIANJI JUZHEN

云南少数民族非纸质典籍聚珍

纳西东巴卷轴画

纳西族源于古代氐羌族群中的古羌人，自称“纳”“纳西”“纳日”“纳恒”等。据2010年第六次全国人口普查统计，纳西族现有326295人，主要聚居在滇、川、藏三省交界的13个区县（丽江市古城区、玉龙、宁蒗、永胜、香格里拉、维西、德钦、贡山、盐源、盐边、木里、芒康、巴塘）境内。

纳西族有自己的语言和文字，纳西语属汉藏语系藏缅语族彝语支，分西部和东部两个方言区。纳西族原有东巴文、哥巴文、阮可文和玛丽玛莎文。东巴文是“唯一活着的象形文字”，常用字有1400多个单字，用东巴文撰写的典籍多达1000余种3万余册。此外，还有少量用哥巴文和阮可文书写的典籍。

纳西族古籍是纳西族传统文化的重要载体，涵盖了用纳西族文字及汉文书写的、反映纳西族历史文化的手稿、文献、文书、谱牒、铭刻以及神话传说、史诗歌谣、民间故事等口传古籍。其中，用纳西族文字书写在特制东巴纸上的东巴古籍体量最大、内容最为丰富，被誉为“纳西族古代社会的百科全书”。按其内容可分为五大类：1. 祈福延寿类。包括祭天、祭祖、祭家神、祭胜利神、祭畜神、祭谷神等。2. 禳鬼消灾类。主要包括抵御灾害，调节是非矛盾，除秽，驱除瘟疫和厄运等内容。3. 丧葬超度类。包括开丧和超度、超度东巴什罗、超度拉姆、祭凶死鬼、大祭风等。4. 占卜类。种类繁多，如《大地上卜卦之书》《用巴格图占卜》《占梦之书》等。5. 杂类。内容涉及舞蹈、医药、民歌等，如《东巴舞谱》《医药之书》《民歌范本》以及独具地域特色的丽江市宁蒗县油米村的阮可东巴经。

纳西族也拥有一定数量的非纸质典籍，大体可分为以下几类：一是铭刻。目前发现的东巴文铭刻存留较少。早在1934年，方国瑜先生在丽江金沙江边的桥头危桥下看到距今约400年的明代哥巴文石刻，刻文大概为“长命永禄”的祈祷词，遗憾此石刻在1951年修路时被毁。此外，在丽江宝山发现过东巴文砖刻，丽江塔城乡还有东巴文墓碑。丽江市博物院便收藏了一些东巴文字砖，东巴文、哥巴文对照印刷雕版等。二是木牌。木牌画纳西语叫“课标”，是为满足祭祀仪式需要，用东巴文和图像在木牌上作画，是一种历史悠久的原始绘画艺术，是东巴艺术在萌芽阶段的产物。三是卷轴画。卷轴画是纳西族古籍的重要组成部分，是蕴含民族历史文化内涵和艺术审美的非纸质典籍，其题材主要反映东巴典籍中的神灵世界和信仰、仪式规程、法事和历算等内容。卷轴画也是纳西族绘画艺术中最原始、最具代表性的艺术形式，是东巴绘画进入快速发展期的产物。元明以后，汉地佛教、道教和藏传佛教相继传入纳西族地区，纳西族绘画进入一个快速发展时期，与汉、藏绘画艺术相结合，特别是唐卡对东巴画产生了较大的影响，纳西族卷轴画在此背景下孕育发展。

卷轴画，纳西语叫“普劳幛”，是东巴用矿物质颜料绘制于土布上的神像画，数量众多，有长卷、多幅和独幅等多种，是东巴绘画艺术跨入发达阶段而趋于精熟的标志。每幅卷轴画主要画一尊大神或护法神，大神画有萨依威德、依古窝格、恒迪窝盘和祖师东巴什罗、药神、战神等，每幅卷轴画表现某个神祇及其所居的神界。画的形式很像唐宋时汉人的佛画尊像，也有明清藏传唐卡的作风。尊像之下，一排为护神力士，最下一排为供养人，尊像底座为莲花座，表现出其与佛教绘画之间的密切关系。卷轴画主要用于东巴教仪式中，悬挂于神坛正上方，不同仪式所挂的神像不尽相同。代表作品有《东巴什罗像》《东巴教大神依古阿格》《战神优麻》《阳神董神、阴神术神》《萨英威德》和神路图等。神路图是东巴卷轴画中极具代表性的巨作。纳西语原名“亨日皮”，意为东巴为死者评断指点去往神地之路，即为亡灵排忧解难，把亡灵从鬼地（地狱）的煎熬中解脱超度出来，在人类之地转生为人，或送至神灵之地。作为长幅布面卷轴画，一般宽 16—30 厘米，长 10—20 米。全卷以分段连续的形式，勾线填色的表现手法，用炭条起稿，按轮廓涂以矿物质或植物制作的颜料，有的调以适量白粉和胶水，然后用毛笔墨线勾勒。神路图主要用于丧葬时超度死者亡灵的仪式，可分为地狱、人间、天堂三个部分，绘有 360 多个人、神、鬼及 70 多种奇禽怪兽，被称为我国美术史上最长的直幅长卷，享有“古代宗教绘画第一长卷”之誉，具有较高的文化和艺术研究价值。

Naqxiceef tee ebbei sherlbbei Di’ qai sel gge zzi’ qu hual loq gge gv’ qai xi gol nee ceeq, wuduwuq “Naq” “Naqxi” “Naqree” “Naqhil” cheehu bbei sel. 2010 N dil luq ceel cuaiqguef sseiqke pvcaf tejil gol nee liuf ceeq mei, Naqxiceef xi eyi tee 326295 gvl jjuq, zeeyal seil Yuiqnaiq, Seelcuai, Sizail chee seelsei gai zulzu gv gge 13 gol quxail loq zzeeq (Liljai sheel Gvceiq qu, Yulleq xail, Liqlail xail, Yeseil xail, Xaigefli’ la xail, Weiqsi xail, Defqi xail, Gulsai xail, Yaiqyuaiq xail, Yaiqbiai xail, Mufli xail, Maiqkai xail, Bataiq xail).

Naqxiceef wuduwuq gge geezheeq nef tei’ ee jju, Naqxi geezheeq chee hailzail yuxil zailmiai yuceef yiqyuzhee loq yi, sibvl faiyaiq nef debvl faiyaiq bbei bbiu. Naqxiceef gge tei’ ee seil dobbaq tei’ ee, ggeqbbaq tei’ ee, rerko tei’ ee, ma’ lil masa tei’ ee lusiuq jju. Dobbaq tei’ ee seil eyi doltv teif zeizeiq neeq gge xailxiq veiqzeel ddeesiuq waq, zeizeiq bbeeq gge tei’ ee zziuq 1400 hal jju, tei’ eezziuq cheehu nee berl teiqji gge dobbaq tei’ ee 3 mee cai hal jju. Ggeqbbaq tei’ ee nef rerko tei’ ee nee berl gge tei’ ee la ddeehu jju.

Naqxi ceef gvzif chee Naqxi ceef ebbeisherlbbei ddeegaiq gge ddumuq ozzei teiq jeldiu mei waq, Naqxi tei’ ee nee berl gge yi, Habaq tei’ ee nee berl gge la yi, sega, veiqxail, veiqsu, pvdif, teiq ddv gge nef seiqhual cuaiqsof, sheeshee, zzerbee, jaibee cheehu nvlku nee mail zul bbel ceeq gge ggvzzei cheehu waq, ddeehe bbei Naqxi ceef gge liqshee veiqhual teiq sel. Ggvzzeiq cheehu loq Naqxi tei’ ee nee teifbif bbei malma bbel ceeq gge seiseel gol teiq berl gge Dobbaq tei’ ee nee bbeeq seiq, sseiddeq dddeebeil gge sher teiq sel yeel, “Naqxiceef gvdail selhuil gge befko cuaiqsu” bbei sel. Tei’ ee loq nee teiq sel gge sher gol nee liu’ liuq bbei bbiu yeel waqsiuq bbei bbiu: 1.Bbibbiq leillei sseesherq halyi yel zherq. Meebiuq, apvzzee sul, seelkvq, ggabiuq, nolbiuq, oqmeibiuq cheehu yi. 2.Sherkuaq bvlbv ceeqderq sul. Sherkua jju me zherq, me hohof sher jju seil selse yel, me gaizil sher bvlbv, gguqkuaq sherzza bvlbv cheehu yi. 3.Xishee ceeqngvl. Xikai xingvl, bvlbv, Sherller ngvl, Lamu ngvl, bbeeqngvl, her’ la’ leeqkeel cheehu yi. 4. Zeezeeq gulgu. Cheezu seil bbeeq ssua, <Ddiuqzeeq> <Bageq zeeq> <Yilmu siuq liuq>

cheehu tei’ ee jju. 5.Holho nolno gge tei’ ee. Chee loq seil comuq, cher’ ee, zzerbee cheehu yi, <Dobbaq comuq> <Cher’ ee tei’ ee> <Zzerbee tei’ ee> nef bifddiuq gol me nilniq gge Liljail sheel Liqlail xail Yeqmi cui gge rerko dobbaq tei’ ee cheehu waq.

Naqxi ceef tee seiseel gol nee berl me waq gge diaizif ddeehu jju mel see, ce ddee ni siuq bbei bbiu tal: ddeesiuq seil teiq ddv gge miqkef. Eyi see gge dobbaq tei’ ee miqkef ddeemaiq nee. 1934 N, Fai Guefyuq seeqzzee nee Liljai Yibbiq ku Qaqteq gge zzoqlvq ddee zzoq bbvq nee, 400 kvl gai Miqdail gge ggeqbbaq tei’ ee nee lvba gol teiq ddv gge sheefkef ddoq, tei’ ee loq “sseesherq halyi” yelhol gge geezheeq teiq berl. Kosif mei sheefkef cheegel 1951 N sseeggv sie cheekaq pielpie bbel hee seiq. Ejuq gge seil Liljai Lvperqwe nee wazheeqbie gol Dobbaq tei’ ee teiq ddv gge ddoq jji, Talzzaiq nee feiqlv gol dobbaq teiq’ ee teiq ddv gge jju. Liljai sheel bof’ vqyuail loq dobbaq tei’ ee ddv gge wazheeqbie, dobbaq tei’ ee, ggeqbbaq tei’ ee duilzal gge yilsuaf diabai cheehu jju. Nisiuq cheesiuq seil kolbbaiqwaq. Kolbbaiq chee habaq geezheeq seil mufpaiqhual bbei sel. Tee chee biubiuq sulsu gv zeiq dder yeel, serpeil gol nee dobbaq tei’ ee nef tvqsiail teiq hual, halsherq gge yuaiqshee huilhual yilsuf ddeesiuq waq. Dobbaq yilsuf gai bie neeq chee rheeq gge ggvzzeiq waq. Seesiuq cheesiuq seil zai waq. Zai chee Naqxi ceef gvzif loq zulyal gge ddeesiuq waq, miqceef liqshee veiqhual gge goqwa nef yilsuf sei mei chee loq yi, seiseel gol berl me waq gge diaizif waq. Zai gol teiq hual gge chee dobbaq jeq loq gge heiqddiuq, biubiuq sulsu ddumuq, zeezzeeq gulgu sher cheehu ko teiq sel. Zai chee Naqxi ceef huilhual yilsuf loq zuil jju cuq, zuil dailbiasil jju gge yilsuf ddeesiuq waq, dobbaq huilhual cuq bbei gai tv chee rheeq gge ggvzzeiq waq. Yuaiq caq nef Miq caq gguq seil, habaq ddiuq gge foqjal, daljal nef Ggvzzeeq ddiuq gge zailcuail foqjal bbei Naqxi ddiuqkol tv, Naqxi ceef gge huilhual la fafzai cuq ddee zherl loq tv, Habaq nef Ggvzzeeq gge huilhual yilsuf gol gai zzeezzeeq, lamaq zai nee dobbaqhual gol gge yixai ddeeq ssua, Naqxi dobbaq zai chee ce bbei bie ceeq sei.

Naqxi gge pv’ laq zai gol Habaq seil juaizuqhual bbei sel, chee tee dobbaq nee lvba gol nee tv gge ssalcher zeiq yeel peiq gol teiq hual gge pv’ laq gol sel, sseiddeq ddeebeil jju, zai sherq, ddeepeil zai nef sseipeil zai cheehu jjaiq nisiuq jju, chee tee dobbaq huilhual yilsuf fafdaf gaiduail loq tv, lahal lahal ee neeq mei waq. Zai ddeepeil gol heiqddeeq ddeezzer mewaf gga’ laq ddeezzer hual, heiqddeeq tee Saqyi weddei, Yiggvq ageq, Heiqddee wo’ perq nef Dibba sherllo, Dogeq, Yemaq cheehu waq, zai ezee ddeepeil megua heiq ddeezzee nef tee nee xul gge heiqddiuq teiq hual. Hual gge xiqsheel seil Habaq Taiqcaq sulcaq cheerheeq gge pv’ laq bie, Miqcaq Cicaq Ggvzzeef gge lamaq zai la bie. Heiqddeeq bbvq, ddee’ lerq seil heiq zahu gge gga’ laq, muftai muftai chee’ lerq seil pv’ laq vqreega, heiq zzeeqgv seil liqhuaq bbaq zzeeqgv, ddaqbaq huilhual gol nvlnv ssua. Dobbaq sherbbei seil zai tee heiqjjiq gge ggeqdol chee, sherbbei me nilniq seil chee gge heiq la me nilniq. Dailbia zofpi seil <Dobbaq ddee Dibba sherller zai> <Dobbaq heiqddeeq Yiggvq ageq zai> <Gga’ laq yemaq zai> <Ddu seiq zai> <Saqyi weddei zai> <Heiq ddee> cheehu jju. Heiq ddee seil dobbaq zai loq zuil yuaiqshee, zuil dailbiasil jju gge sherddeeq gge zofpi waq, Naqxi geezheeq seil “heiqreepiq” sel, <Heiqddee>cheeheireepiq, heiqreepucheekaqzeiq. Xi sheepilseildobbaq nee heiqddiuqbbeeggesseeggv lei zheeyel, xi sheecheegvlzzeebbeisherperq, tee ggeoqheicheeniweceiqholddiuq neeggeqlei sherl beelceeq,bbeiceeqsseeggeddiuq lei tv,me wafmeqzeelbvlbvbbelheiqddiuqtvheezherq. <Heiqddee> tee tobvlgol nee hualggezaisherqwaq, yifbaibaqnv 16-30 liqmi, sherqnv 10-20 liqmi. Zaicheepeilzherlbbiunal lei zulzu, keeqbbaqhual, ssalcher keel, fvljji nee gaihual, mailgguqseillvbanefzzerqgol nee tvggessalcher keel, ddeehuseilperqchernef biqddeemaiqzeiq, bbilseilmaqbif nee keeqbbaqge. <Heiqddee>cheexisheexingvlsherb beicheekaqzeiqbbeeq, niweceiqholddiuq, xi ddiuq, heiqddiuqseelddiuqbbiu, xi, heiq, ceeq 360 gvlhalnefddvzzeeqkozzeeq 70 siuqhalteiqhual. Ngelggeeqguefjameisufshee golzuilsherqggezaibbeisel, “ebbeisherlbbeizujalhuilhualdilyifcaiqjuail” selmiqzzeeq, veiqhualnefyilsufyaijelgol nee selseiljjaiqbbeiqpvseiq.

恒底沃盘

年代：清代

尺寸：140cm × 60cm

收藏单位：丽江市博物院

萨依威德大神
年代：清代
尺寸：95cm × 46cm
收藏单位：丽江市东巴文化研究院

萨依威德大神
年代：清代
尺寸：140cm×56cm
收藏单位：丽江市东巴文化研究院

萨依威德大神

年代：清代

尺寸：86cm × 48cm

收藏单位：丽江市东巴文化研究院

萨依威德大神
年代：清代
尺寸：86cm × 48cm
收藏单位：丽江市东巴文化研究院

东巴什罗
年代：明代
尺寸：60cm × 48cm
收藏单位：丽江市东巴文化研究院

东巴什罗

年代：清代

尺寸：89cm×63.5cm

收藏单位：丽江市东巴文化研究院

东巴什罗
年代：清代
尺寸：140cm × 86cm
收藏单位：丽江市玉龙纳西族自治县图书馆

东巴什罗
年代：清代
尺寸：110cm × 55cm
收藏单位：丽江市东巴文化研究院

东巴什罗
年代：清代
尺寸：88cm × 60cm
收藏单位：丽江市玉龙纳西族自治县图书馆

东巴什罗
年代：清代
尺寸：116cm × 59cm
收藏单位：丽江市东巴文化研究院

东巴什罗
年代：清代
尺寸：62cm × 45cm
收藏单位：丽江市玉龙纳西族自治县图书馆

东巴什罗
年代：清代
尺寸：86cm × 47cm
收藏单位：丽江市玉龙纳西族自治县图书馆

谷神"诺妥沈"
年代：清代
尺寸：52cm × 43cm
收藏单位：丽江市玉龙纳西族自治县图书馆

谷神“诺妥沈”
年代：清代
尺寸：62cm×43cm
收藏单位：丽江市玉龙纳西族自治县图书馆

谷神"诺妥沈"
年代：清代
尺寸：68cm × 41cm
收藏单位：丽江市玉龙纳西族自治县图书馆

谷神“诺妥沈”

年代：清代

尺寸：116cm×46cm

收藏单位：丽江市东巴文化研究院

众神图
年代：清代
尺寸：84cm × 64cm
收藏单位：丽江市玉龙纳西族自治县图书馆

众神图
年代：清代
尺寸：116cm×85cm
收藏单位：丽江市玉龙纳西族自治县图书馆

众神图
年代：清代
尺寸：100cm × 75cm
收藏单位：丽江市玉龙纳西族自治县图书馆

盘孜沙美女神
年代：清代
尺寸：26cm × 165cm
收藏单位：丽江市玉龙纳西族自治县图书馆

盘孜沙美女神

年代：清代

尺寸：23cm×57cm

收藏单位：丽江市玉龙纳西族自治县图书馆

沈神和卢神

年代：清代

尺寸：122cm × 21cm

收藏单位：丽江市博物院

沈神和卢神
年代：清代
尺寸：93cm × 27cm
收藏单位：丽江市玉龙纳西族自治县图书馆

三多神与城隍神
年代：清代
尺寸：104cm × 60cm
收藏单位：丽江市玉龙纳西族自治县图书馆

格控战神
年代：清代
尺寸：77cm × 47cm
收藏单位：丽江市玉龙纳西族自治县图书馆

格控战神
年代：清代
尺寸：93cm × 56cm
收藏单位：丽江市玉龙纳西族自治县图书馆

格控战神

年代：民国

尺寸：131cm × 64cm

收藏单位：丽江市东巴文化研究院

格控战神
年代：清代
尺寸：75cm×52cm
收藏单位：丽江市玉龙纳西族自治县图书馆

格控战神

年代：清代

尺寸：68cm × 52cm

收藏单位：丽江市东巴文化研究院

朗究敬究战神

年代：清代

尺寸：70cm × 49cm

收藏单位：丽江市玉龙纳西族自治县图书馆

朗究敬究战神

年代：清代

尺寸：63cm × 50cm

收藏单位：丽江市玉龙纳西族自治县图书馆

朗究敬究战神

年代：清代

尺寸：55cm × 42cm

收藏单位：丽江市玉龙纳西族自治县图书馆

朗究敬究战神
年代：清代
尺寸：63cm×50cm
收藏单位：丽江市玉龙纳西族自治县图书馆

朗究敬究战神
年代：清代
尺寸：97cm × 65cm
收藏单位：丽江市东巴文化研究院

麦布精如战神
年代：清代
尺寸：117cm × 62cm
收藏单位：丽江市玉龙纳西族自治县图书馆

卡冉战神
年代：清代
尺寸：89cm×57cm
收藏单位：丽江市玉龙纳西族自治县图书馆

卡冉战神

年代：清代

尺寸：77cm×60cm

收藏单位：丽江市玉龙纳西族自治县图书馆

卡冉战神
年代：清代
尺寸：68cm × 56cm
收藏单位：丽江市玉龙纳西族自治县图书馆

卡冉战神
年代：清代
尺寸：71cm×57cm
收藏单位：丽江市玉龙纳西族自治县图书馆

卡冉战神
年代：清代
尺寸：125cm × 48cm
收藏单位：丽江市东巴文化研究院

卡冉战神

年代：民国

尺寸：100cm × 64cm

收藏单位：丽江市东巴文化研究院

瑞格战神

年代：清代

尺寸：80cm × 46cm

收藏单位：丽江市玉龙纳西族自治县图书馆

帽米巴拉
年代：清代
尺寸：52cm × 38cm
收藏单位：丽江市玉龙纳西族自治县图书馆

帕米巴拉

年代：民国

尺寸：90cm × 46cm

收藏单位：丽江市东巴文化研究院

大鹏神鸟
年代：清代
尺寸：98cm × 45cm
收藏单位：丽江市东巴文化研究院

五方修曲大鹏
年代：清代
尺寸：65cm × 40cm
收藏单位：丽江市玉龙纳西族自治县图书馆

大鹏神鸟
年代：清代
尺寸：71cm × 45cm
收藏单位：丽江市玉龙纳西族自治县图书馆

孟时优麻

年代：清代

尺寸：87cm × 46cm

收藏单位：丽江市玉龙纳西族自治县图书馆

扭扭优麻战神
年代：清代
尺寸：73cm × 53cm
收藏单位：丽江市玉龙纳西族自治县图书馆

扭扭优麻战神、佐体优麻战神
年代：清代
尺寸：55cm × 42cm
收藏单位：丽江市博物院

扭扭优麻战神
年代：清代
尺寸：106cm×78.5cm
收藏单位：丽江市东巴文化研究院

佐体优麻战神

年代：清代

尺寸：74cm × 45cm

收藏单位：丽江市玉龙纳西族自治县图书馆

佐体优麻战神
年代：清代
尺寸：88cm × 50cm
收藏单位：丽江市玉龙纳西族自治县图书馆

佐体优麻战神

年代：清代

尺寸：77cm × 51cm

收藏单位：丽江市玉龙纳西族自治县图书馆

佐体优麻战神
年代：清代
尺寸：102cm × 51cm
收藏单位：丽江市东巴文化研究院

突赤优麻战神
年代：清代
尺寸：71cm × 45cm
收藏单位：丽江市玉龙纳西族自治县图书馆

巴乌优麻战神
年代：清代
尺寸：85cm × 63cm
收藏单位：丽江市玉龙纳西族自治县图书馆

突赤优麻战神
年代：清代
尺寸：70cm × 54cm
收藏单位：丽江市玉龙纳西族自治县图书馆

优麻战神
年代：清代
尺寸：78cm×57cm
收藏单位：丽江市玉龙纳西族自治县图书馆

巴乌优麻战神
年代：清代
尺寸：123cm × 45cm
收藏单位：丽江市东巴文化研究院

优麻战神
年代：清代
尺寸：74cm × 64cm
收藏单位：丽江市东巴文化研究院

青龙与黄龙
年代：清代
尺寸：119cm × 25cm
收藏单位：丽江市玉龙纳西族自治县图书馆

绿龙

年代：清代

尺寸：96cm × 28cm

收藏单位：丽江市玉龙纳西族自治县图书馆

青龙与绿龙
年代：清代
尺寸：110cm × 29cm
收藏单位：丽江市玉龙纳西族自治县图书馆

青龙与绿龙

年代：清代

尺寸：104cm × 28cm

收藏单位：丽江市玉龙纳西族自治县图书馆

青龙
年代：清代
尺寸：120cm × 22cm
收藏单位：丽江市玉龙纳西族自治县图书馆

青龙
年代：清代
尺寸：119cm × 29cm
收藏单位：丽江市玉龙纳西族自治县图书馆

神路图

神路图（一）
年代：民国
尺寸：1140cm × 35cm
收藏单位：丽江市玉龙纳西族自治县图书馆

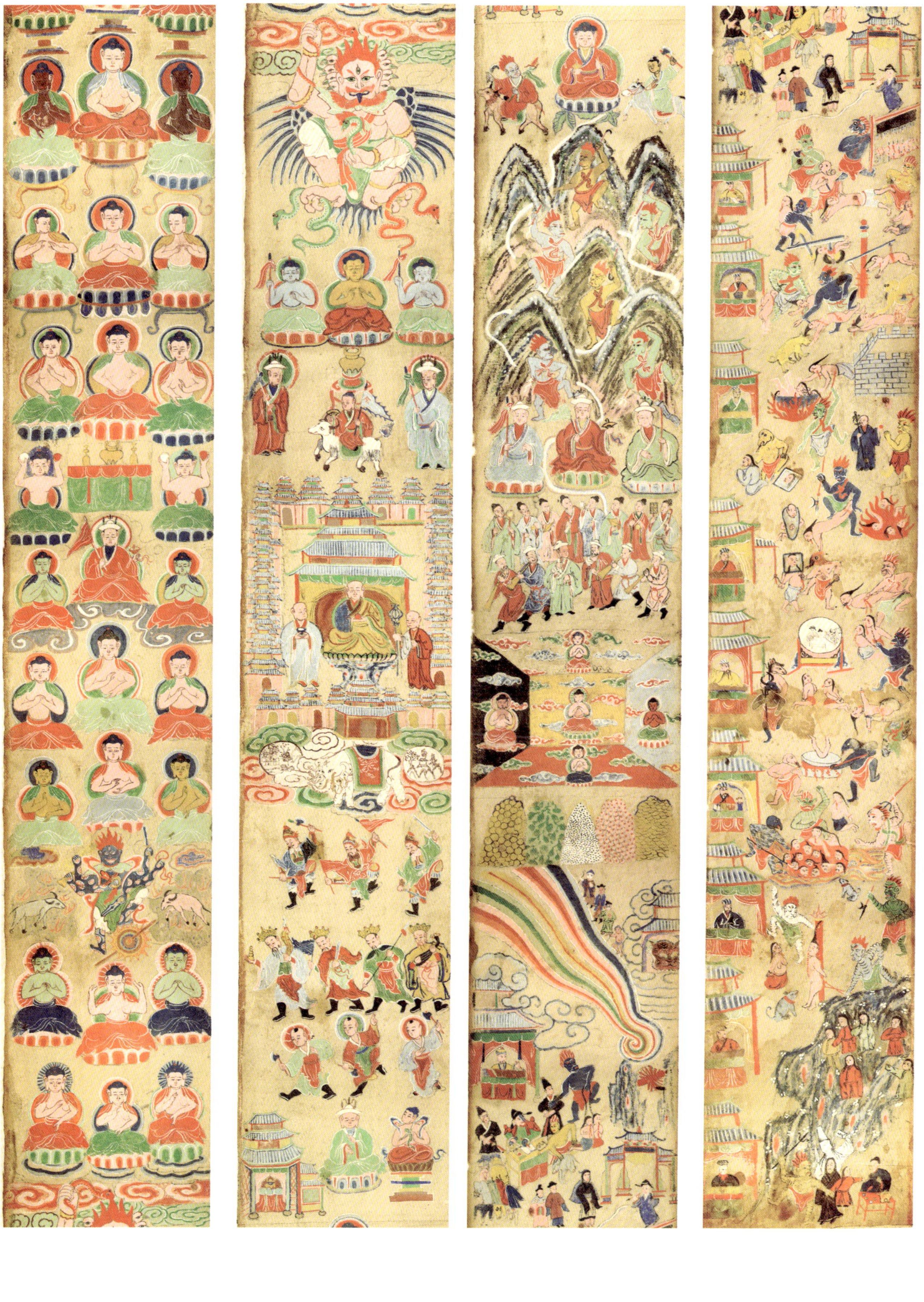

神路图（二）
年代：清代
尺寸：583cm × 29cm
收藏单位：丽江市玉龙纳西族自治县图书馆

神路图（三）

年代：清代

尺寸：1067cm × 25cm

收藏单位：丽江市玉龙纳西族自治县图书馆

说明：此神路图材质较特殊，卷首为麻布，中部拼接土纸，因较为罕见，故收录在此。

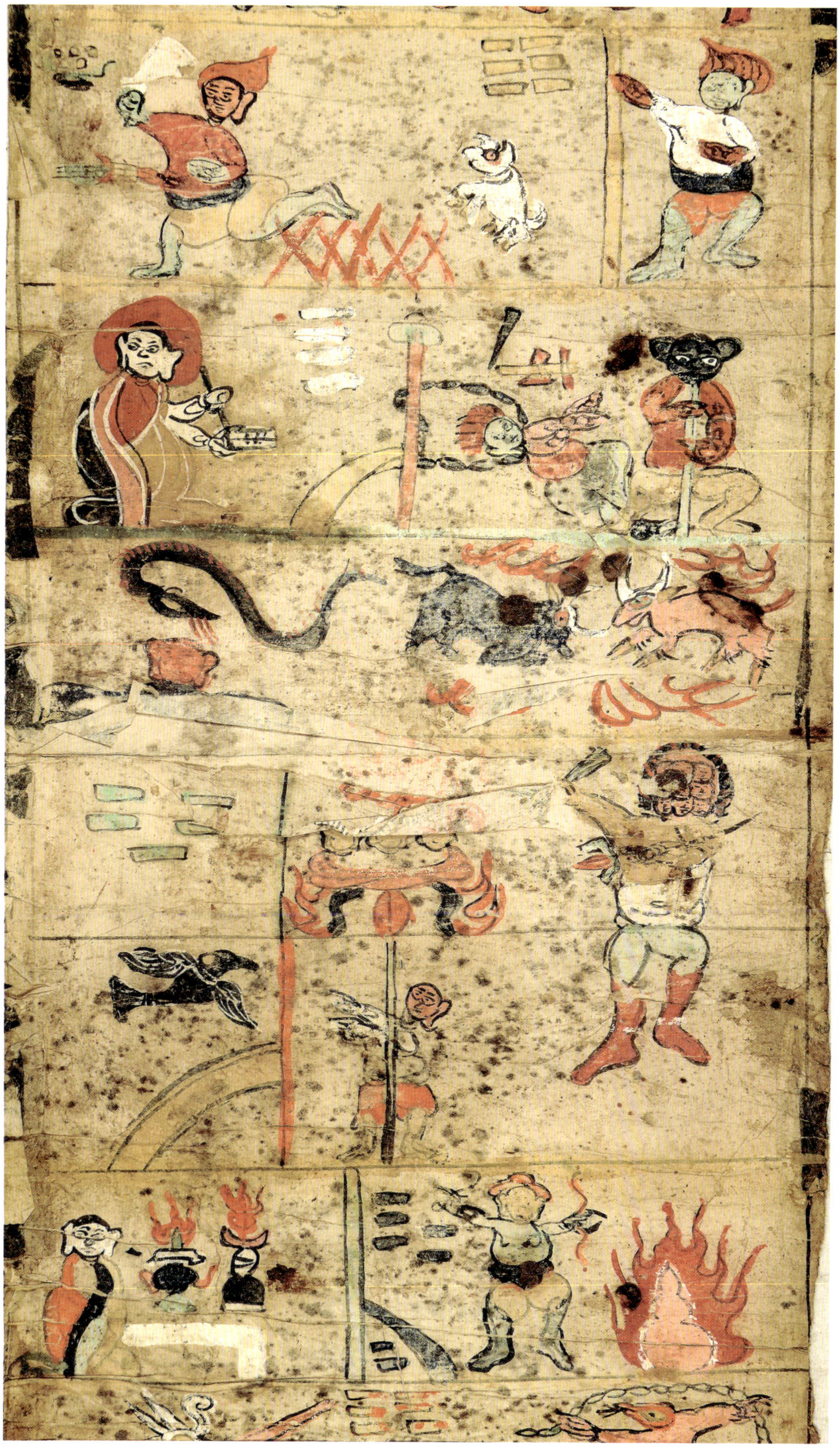

神路图（四）
年代：清代
尺寸：334cm × 23cm
收藏单位：丽江市玉龙纳西族自治县图书馆

神路图（五）
年代：清代
尺寸：1067cm × 25cm
收藏单位：丽江市博物院

萬年燈

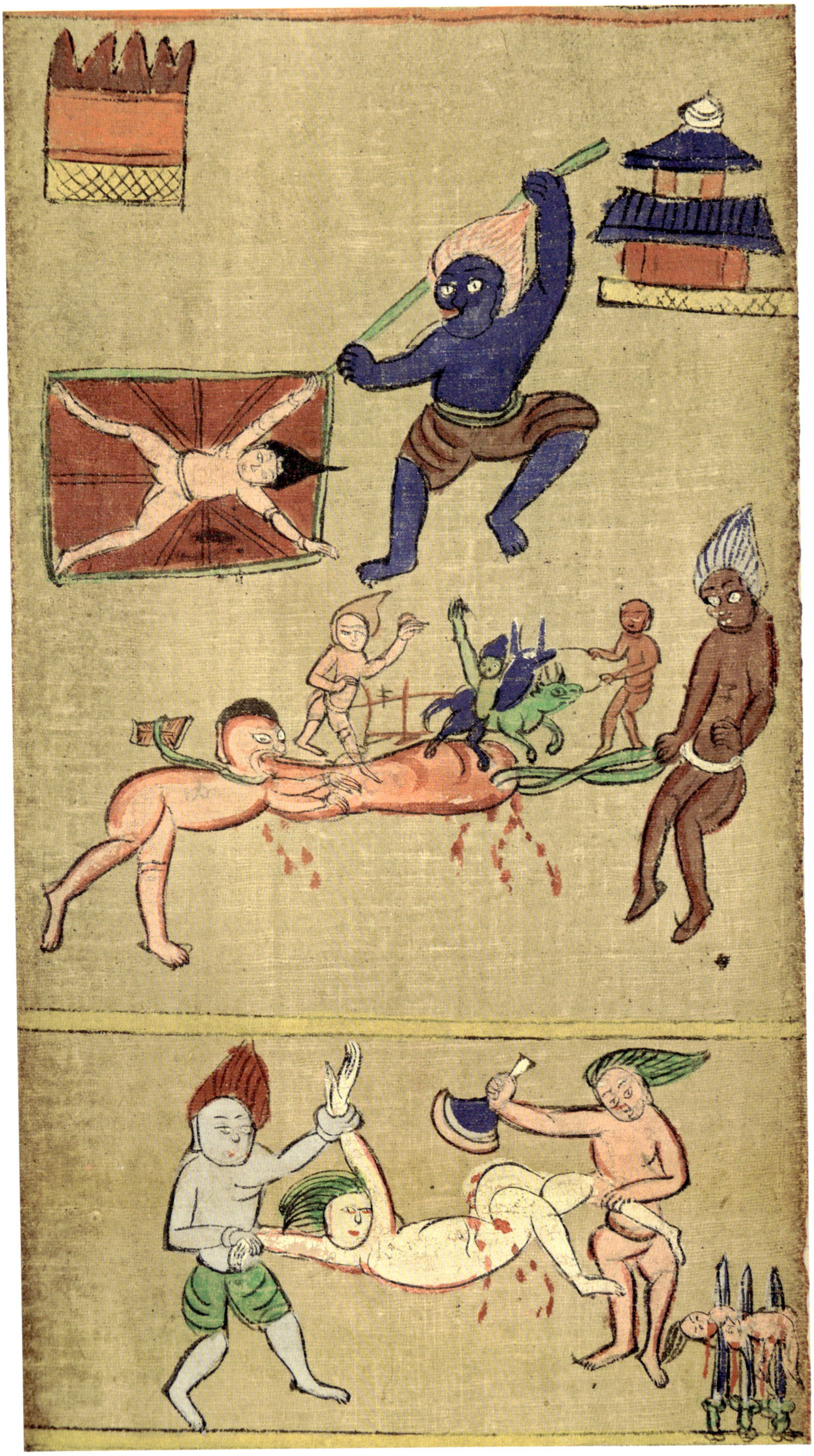

YUNNAN SHAOSHU MINZU
FEIZHIZHI DIANJI JUZHEN

云南少数民族非纸质典籍聚珍

壮族神图长卷

壮族是我国岭南一带的土著民族，由古代越人的一支发展而来，与周秦时期的西瓯、骆越，汉唐的俚、僚、越、濮、乌浒，宋以后的僮人、良人、仲家、土人等有密切的族源关系。

历史上，自称复杂、因地因时而异，有“夷越”“夷濮”“濮依”“布爽”“布壮”“仲家”“沙人”“土人”等20余种。1949年以后，按本民族意愿，统称“僮族”。1965年，经国务院批准，改称“壮族”。壮族是我国人口最多的少数民族，据2010年人口普查，全国有1900余万，集中分布于广西壮族自治区和云南省，广东、贵州和湖南有少量分布。云南省现有壮族人口近120万，主要分布在文山壮族苗族自治州和红河哈尼族彝族自治州。

壮族有自己的语言文字，壮语属汉藏语系壮侗语族壮傣语支，分南北两大方言。壮族文字在先秦时期即已萌芽，今壮族分布区尚存数百处摩崖刻画。隋唐时期，壮族先民即用汉字记壮语，效仿汉字六书的构字方法创制了方块壮字，称“土字”或“土俗字”，并用古壮字来记录民间故事，书写经文、家谱、碑文、账务等，一批方块壮字古籍流传至今。古壮文古籍，壮语称“师摩”“师多在”“师雅”等，“师”壮语意为“书籍”，多抄写在用纱皮树树皮制成的纱纸上，或是用嫩竹、构树皮制成的者卡土纸上。壮族纸质古籍种类广、数量多，有记录摩教仪式、经文、教义的《摩布洛陀》《摩荷泰》《麻仙》《德傣掸登俄》等，有反映朴素世界观和价值观的叙事长诗、古歌，如《盘古歌》《卜伯》《摩则杜》等，有民间七言叙事诗《毛洪》《董永》《舜儿》等，亦不乏展现绘画艺术的《鸡卜经》及宗教绘画“莱摩”，内容涉及历史、语言、文学、艺术、哲学、宗教、天文、历算、美术等众多方面，可谓博大精深、绮丽多姿。

壮族信奉原始的摩教，崇拜祖先，崇尚自然，为满足宗教需要，摩教祭司“博摩”（男祭司）和“乜满”（女祭司）绘制了一系列配合摩经使用的宗教画，并传承至今，壮语称之为“莱摩”。壮族的“莱摩”绘画载体丰富多样、形制各异，有绘制于土麻布之上的神图长卷，有绘制于土纸上的宗教神像挂画，还有绘制于纸质文献《鸡卜经》里的占卜绘画。“莱摩”绘画作品以神像画居多，人物形象根据民间神话传说塑造，没有特定的形象作为标准，一般根据绘画的功用和人们的审美习惯，以人的基本形态为基础，采用适度合理的夸张变形的艺术手法进行创作。这类绘画兼具艺术和实用性，带有浓厚的宗教色彩和功利性，隐含借“神”避邪的世俗观念，审美态度与情感交织，又反映出文化的交流与交融。

神图长卷是壮族最具代表性的非纸质典籍之一。摩教神图长卷，又称“摩教铭旌神图长卷”，是摩教特有的宗教神图之一，由摩教祭司传承使用。神图绘于壮家自制土麻布上，形制为长卷竖幅，分栏作画，每栏是一个相对独立的图幅，又不失整体联系。上面绘有大王之祖（布洛陀）、王（召领）、神（日、月、雷、水等）、人、动物以及战争、交媾、祭祀、劳作、划船等内容，是一幅展现祭拜祖先神灵、祈福纳祥、求六畜兴旺、伦理道德宣教的画卷。神图长卷多用于丧葬仪式、祭扫仪式等。仪式过程中，祭司需悬挂神图长卷并吟诵“摩经”，祈求神灵的保佑，实现举行仪式的目的。每幅画面都有相应的“摩经”作解。如现由麻栗坡县八布乡竜龙村“布摩”张庭会收藏的摩教神图长卷，长 2.9 米、宽 0.23 米，共有图案（竖幅）22 幅，举行扫家仪式时，祭司在仪式活动中悬挂此神图并吟诵摩经《故版壬》。

此外，壮族宗教祭司“博摩”作为地域宗教群体的代表者、传承者、执行者和人神沟通的使者，仪式过程中要穿法衣、戴法帽、执法器，以此体现庄严的身份并营造一种特殊的宗教氛围。“博摩”的法衣、法冠上大多绘有布洛陀、召领、日、月、雷、水、人、动物以及战争、交媾、祭祀等内容，以此祈求神灵庇佑、赐予灵力。法衣、戴法帽、执法器等物件上所绘制的符号或图案，具有特殊的文化涵义，是壮族摩教文化的重要组成部分。从广义的层面看，也可将其纳入非纸质典籍研究的范畴。

Pujnoengz (bouxcuengh) zawh pujzoeg tiu fang dawj hienz haij Goh raeuz cinh yuq haenj,loh ngah pujveh zohnduq lux raengh maz,daj bungx Cizngaeuz、Lohveh mbongj Zaeuzchauh Qinhchauh,puj Lix、pujraeuz、pujyoij、pujpuh、Uzfuz mbongj Hanqchauh Tanghchauh,pujzoengx、pujlieng、pujzungq、pujdaez gaq mbongj Sungqchauh maz haenj zawh pujzoeg dungzrangh nyaed zawz.Zwznduq,zwh ruangx haeg miz laizawz、yuq dih mboq lumj ruangx mboq lumj,miz “Yihyoij” “Yihpuh” “Pujnoengz” “Baeuhcoengx” “Baeuhzoengx” “Pujzungq” “Pujyoij” “Pujdaeuz” le ngihsip lai yengh naeh.Bi 1949 yaq, yiq goenz pujzoeg zahgaeuq nwh niz,ruangx baenz “Baeuhzoengx” , bi 1965,hawj Gohvuqvienq gangz dingh yaq,dauh ruangx hoek “Bouxcuengh” . Bouhcuengh zawh pujzoeg goenz nuaix miz goenz lai nyiuz Goh raeuz, yi bi 2010 tuam laiz,daengzmowngz miz tiang lux laeng gaeuj baeg lai fanh goenz, tuam yuq Guangxciz bouxcuengh Zwqzwqqiz daj Vinhnanhswnx,Guangxdungz、Goiqzaeuz daj Fuhnanh goj miz mbangj goenz yuq.Vinhnanhswnx gaunaeh miz goenz bouxcuengh zaek taeng baegngih fanh,nauxlai zawh yuq Vwnhcanz Zaeuz bouxcuengh pujmyaux haeg guanj haenj daj Hunghhoh Zaeuz puj haznih pujmowng haeg guanj haenj.

Bouxcuengz haeg miz gaemzkauq tasw zahgaeuq,kauq bouxcuengz zawh ngah kauq bouxcuengz pujdaez zoeg kauq bouxcuengh pujdungq sai kauq pujhaeg pujzangq,baen hoek fang dawj fang now song yengh kauq.Tasw bouxcuengh yuq to mbongj Qinhchauh zoq qix meq yaj,gaunaeh dih bouxcuengh yuq haenj nwngz miz jiq baeg dih va ked ndanq pya.Mbongj Souhchauh Tanghchauh,buqyah bouxcuengh zoq aeu sw haeg laiz nyien kauq bouxcuengh, zaep choek yengh daeuq hoek tasw pujhaeg haenj hoek baenz sw bouxcuengh yaj, ruangx hoek “Sw mbanj” majhax “Sw ndiip” , nwngz aeu sw bouxcuengh zohnduq maz laiz nyien saeh liuz ka’ mbanj,laiz sw mo、sw mingh、sw boi、zaij jienz lenaeh,miz sw nyien zohnduq aeu tasw bouxcuengh laiz haenj liuz taeng gaunaeh lai.Sw nyien zohnduq aeu tasw bouxcuengh laiz haenj,kauq bouxcuengh ruangx “Sw mo” “Sw nduk zaeq” “Sw yah” lenaeh, “sw” ,kauq bouxcuengh zawh hax “Buksw” ,nauxlai laiz yuq now sa jiqka aeu maexdiz uanq daj naeng maexsa hoek baenz haenj, sa Jijkaj zawh gaeq mowngz dih bouxcuengh yuq haeg miz lai, sa ngaeuxlangh kauchaeg、lumh maz nungj uanq,dingz ndaej yaij、dingz ndaej moed,aeu ndaej ndowj zawz.Sw nyien zohnduq bouxcuengh miz lai yengh、rangh laeb lai, miz le《Mo buqloegdoz》《Mo hoektaeq》《Ma sien》《Dowjndaij sanx nden voh》nyien laiz hoekrawz hoekmo、sw mo、mo dijgaeng haenj,miz lownx damz saeh、lownx zohnduq hoekrawz ngangh ndinfax daj hoekrawz ngangh zaqjienz haenj,lumj《Lownx goeknduq》《Pujbowh》《Mo zwznduq》lenaeh,miz lownx gangz saeh liuz ka' mbanj haenj,goj nwngz miz《Sw nduk zaeq》baiz oeg mbaedmungz laizva haenj daj laizva"Laiz mo", ndaw dix hax taeng laeh zoh、gaemzkauq、laizsw、luangh lownx、Zowhcoh、ngangh fax、naeb' anq、laizva le gahlit gahlaeb,hax baenz zawh tuam lai kaeuj ndaek、laizgit laizgyauh.

Bouxcuengh zaw sinq yengh mo zohnduq laeh maz haenj,gih mbod buqyah,zaw zaemz yengh haeg miz,cho hawj hoekmo aeu doh, "Baeuhmo" daj "Yahmaed" va baenz mbaw laizva mwh hoekmo aeu hoj haenj,nwngz laeb daeb taeng gaunaeh,kauq noengz ruangx dix hoek "Laizmo". Yengh va "Laizmo" bouxcuengh miz laizawz、hunq mboq dungzlumj,miz mbaw laizva dijsien riz va yuq now paeng haeg daemq haenj,miz mbaw laizva huaij siengq dijsien hoekmo riz va yuq now sa haeg hoek haenj,nwngz miz laizva naeb zwz va yuq ndaw《Sw ndukzaeq》aeu sa laiz haenj.Yengh va"Laizmo"siengq dijsien miz nauxlai,hunq dijgoenz yi saeh liuz ka' mbanj maz laiz hoek,mboq miz yengh hunq gaeng sej ngan haenj dang zawh yengh yi, nauxlai yi laizva aeu hoek gaeng daj goenzlai gienq hoekrawz dingh yawz haenj,aeu rangh dijgoenz dang goeklaeg,dauh kae naux zawz bej hunq naux hojtiu maz va hoek.Sownh yengh laizva naeh ngangh goj baenz aeu goj baenz,ngaeux doeb miz yengh hoekmo daj kaiswx laizawz,tuam miz zaw dex "Dijsien" viag dijpi yaj,zawh dingh yawz daj zaemz yawz dungzgaeb,hax oeg Vwnhhuaq dungzlaeh daj dungzchuanj mawq.Mbaw laizva dijsien riz zawh yengh laizva zwznduq mboq aeu sa va haenj,naux daeb hax zawh gaiq bouxcuengh nyiuz.

Mbaw laizva dijsien riz zawh yengh laizva zohnduq mboq aeu sa va haenj,naux daeb ndaej zawh gaiq bouxcuengh nyiuz.Mbaw laizva hoekmo riz,goj ruangx"mbaw hoekmo mai minx goenz vaih riz",zawh mbaw laizva hoekmo haeg miz lux,hawj goenz hoekho laeb daeb aeu.Mbaw laizva va yuq now paeng bouxcuengh haeg daemq haenj,rangh dix zawh mbaw riz daengj swh,baen baenz gongh hoek va,gah gongh haeg zawh hunq va lux,goj daj daengz mbaw dungzrangh hoj.Now dix va miz tosaeq buqyah（Buqloegdoz）、hongz（zaeuj lingz）、dijsien（taeuqhoenz、aenhai、faxumj、naemx lenaeh）、dijgoenz、daihdo daj dungzsaeuh、dungz' aeu、baiz mbod、hoekgaengx、vaed lowz le sownh naeh,zawh mbaw laizva baiz oeg mbod buqyah dijsien、nguangz ndae deq yawz、vanz daihdo faed raengh、rux lix hoek ndae haenj.Mbaw laizva riz nauxlai yuq mwh piuj goenz、baet mbanj baet ronz aeu hoj,mwh hoekmo,pujmo aeu huaij mbaw laizva riz nwngz damz "Sw mo",vanz dijsien bauj hoj, venj hoekmo zux vaeh hax hoek ndaej taeng,gah mbaw laizva gaz miz "sw mo" maz hax singj.Lumj mbaw laizva hoekmo riz gaunaeh hawj Zangz Tinhhuiq goenz mbanj Lunghlong Bahbuq Ciengz goek taeq cau liux haenj,riz 2.9 Mix、gangj 0.23 Mix,daengzle miz hunq va（mbaw daengj）ngihsip ngih mbaw,mwh baetronz,pujmo yuq mwh mo haenj huaij mbaw laizva naeh nwngz damz《Guq baetronz》.

Yaq niz, "Baeuh mo" puj hoekmo bouxcuengh dang zawh puj daeb、puj laeb daeb、puj yi hoek bungx hoekmo dinghmowngz goenz zawx hawj dijgoenz dijsien dungzlaeh haenj,mwh hoekmo aeu nungh sowj mo、taemj duz mo、tw vanqnaemx lenaeh,hoekvienj hax oeg dix zawh goenz miz najta nwngz hoek oeg zawh hoekmo yuq haeg miz lux. Now sowj mo、duz mo "Baeuh mo" va miz Buqloegdoz、zaeuj lingz、taeuqhoenz、aenhai、faxumj、naemx、dijgoenz、daihdo daj dungzsaeuh、dungz' aeu、baiz mbod le naeh,hoekvenj aeu maz vanz dijsien bauj ndaej、aeu hawj riangz sien.Yengh mai maj hunqva now sowj mo、duz mo、aen hoekmo le zahoq naeh va haenj,haeg aem miz yengh hax dix,zawh gaiq daeuq baenz yengh mo bouxcuengh daehnaek haenj.Loh laeb laeh gangj maz ngaeux,caeu dix maz dang zawh yengh laizva zwznduq mboq aeu sa va haenj nduanj hoek gojndaej.

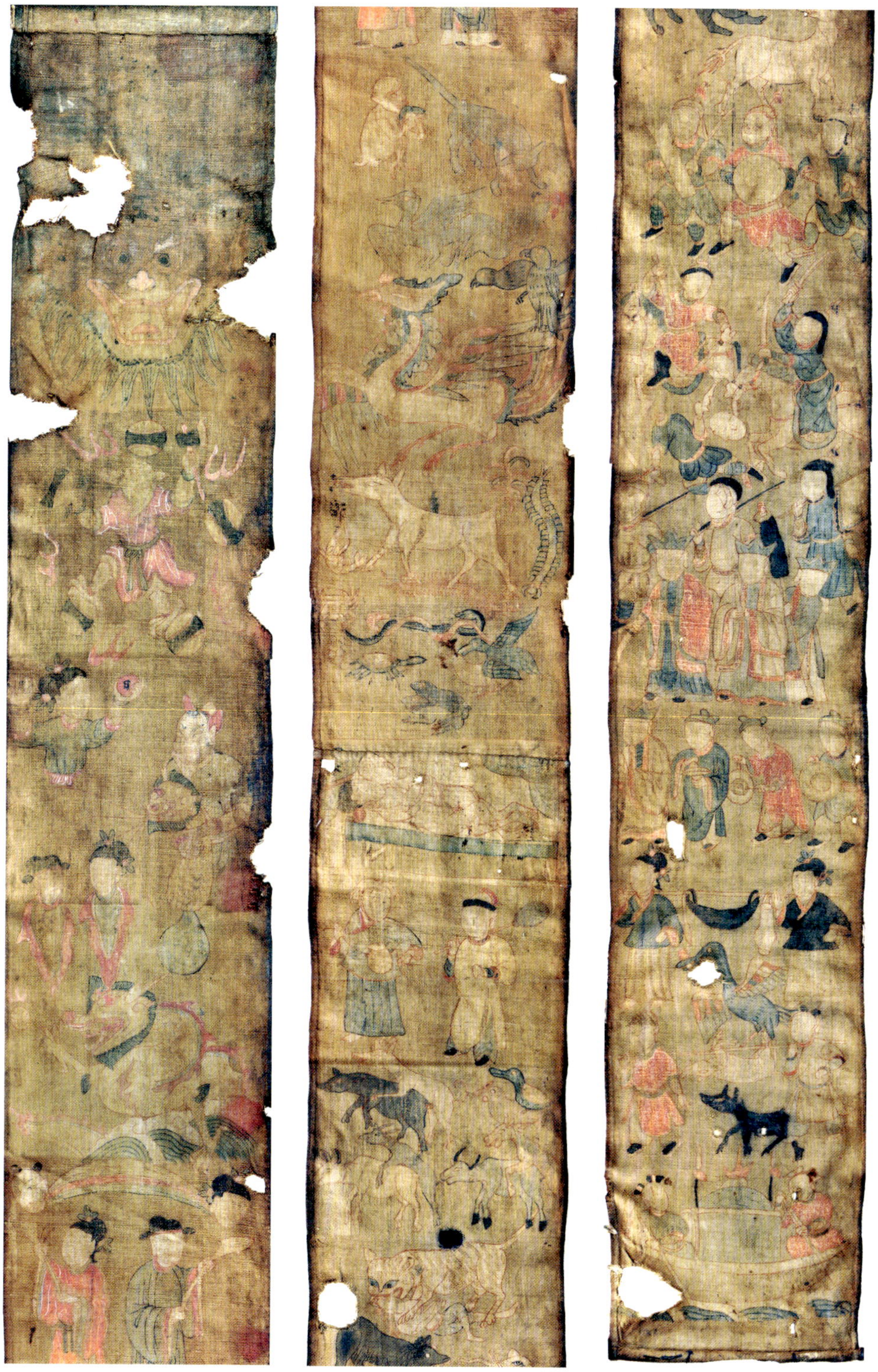

神图长卷（一）
年代：清代
尺寸：300cm × 20cm
收藏者：王明富

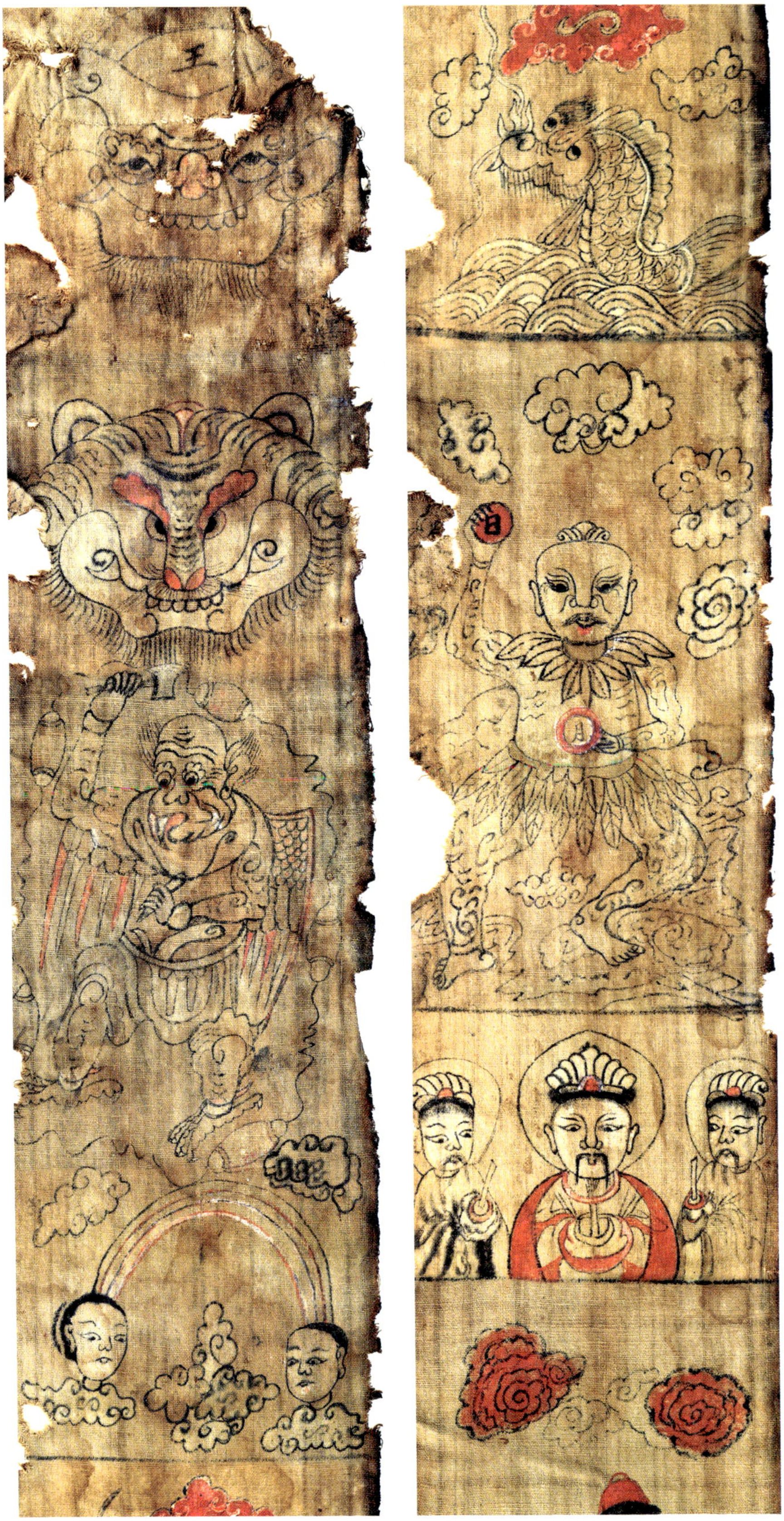

神图长卷（二）
年代：清代
尺寸：300cm × 20cm
收藏者：龙纪峰

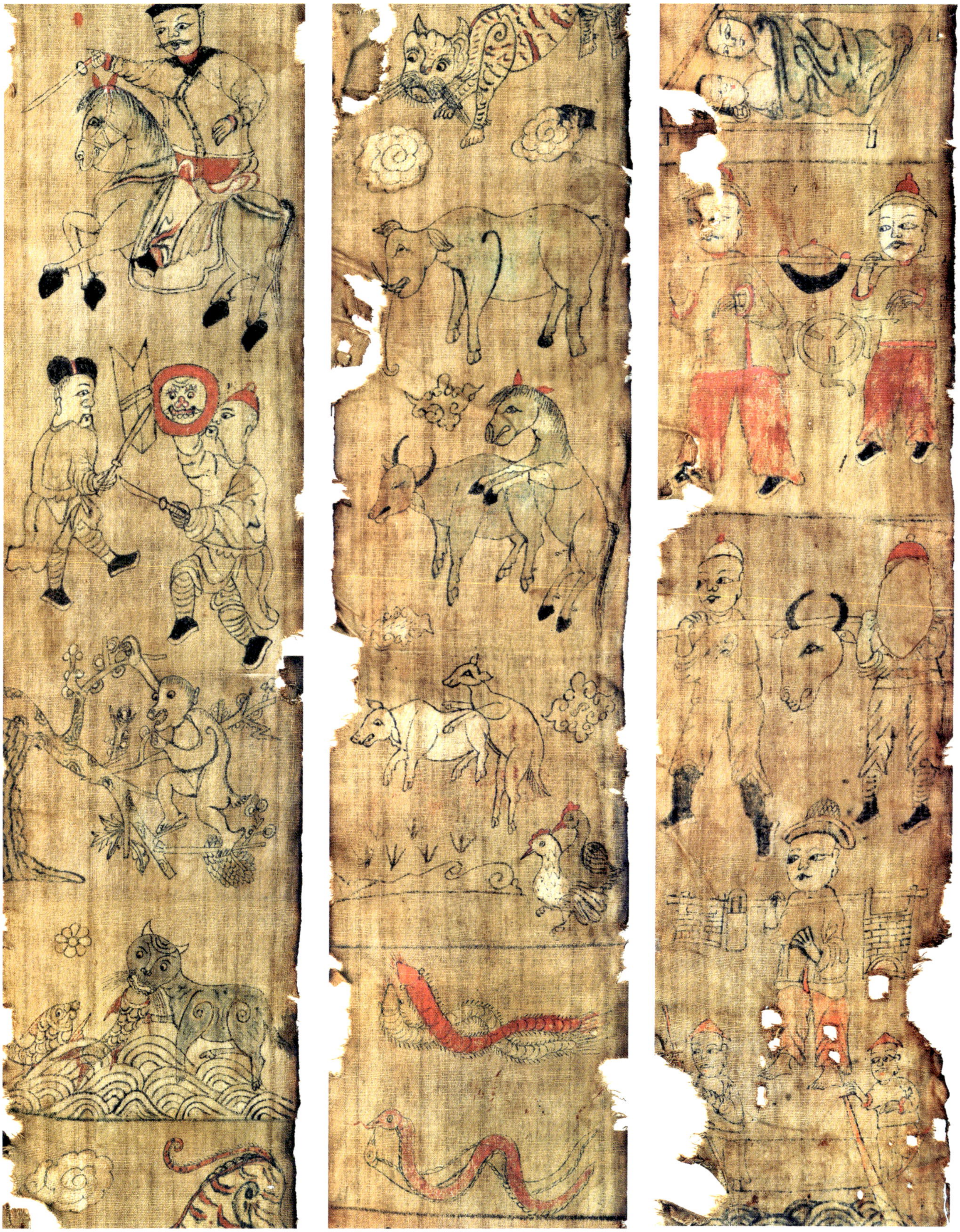

日
月

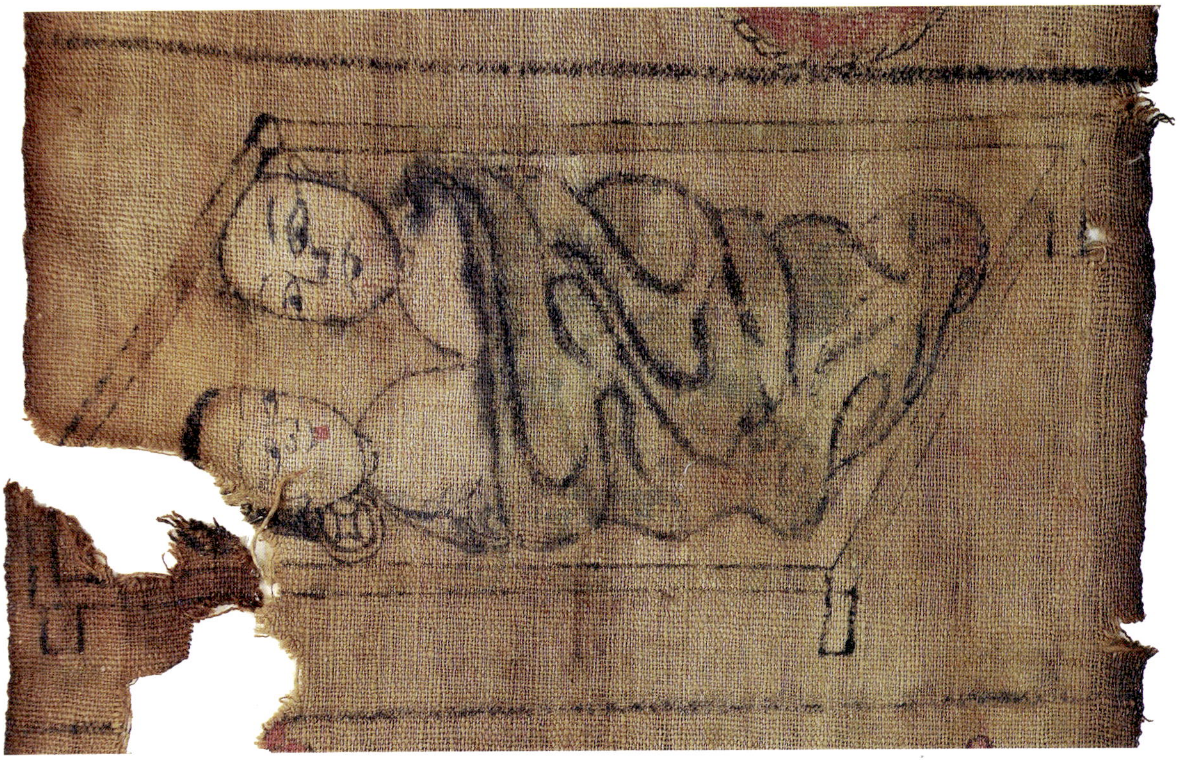

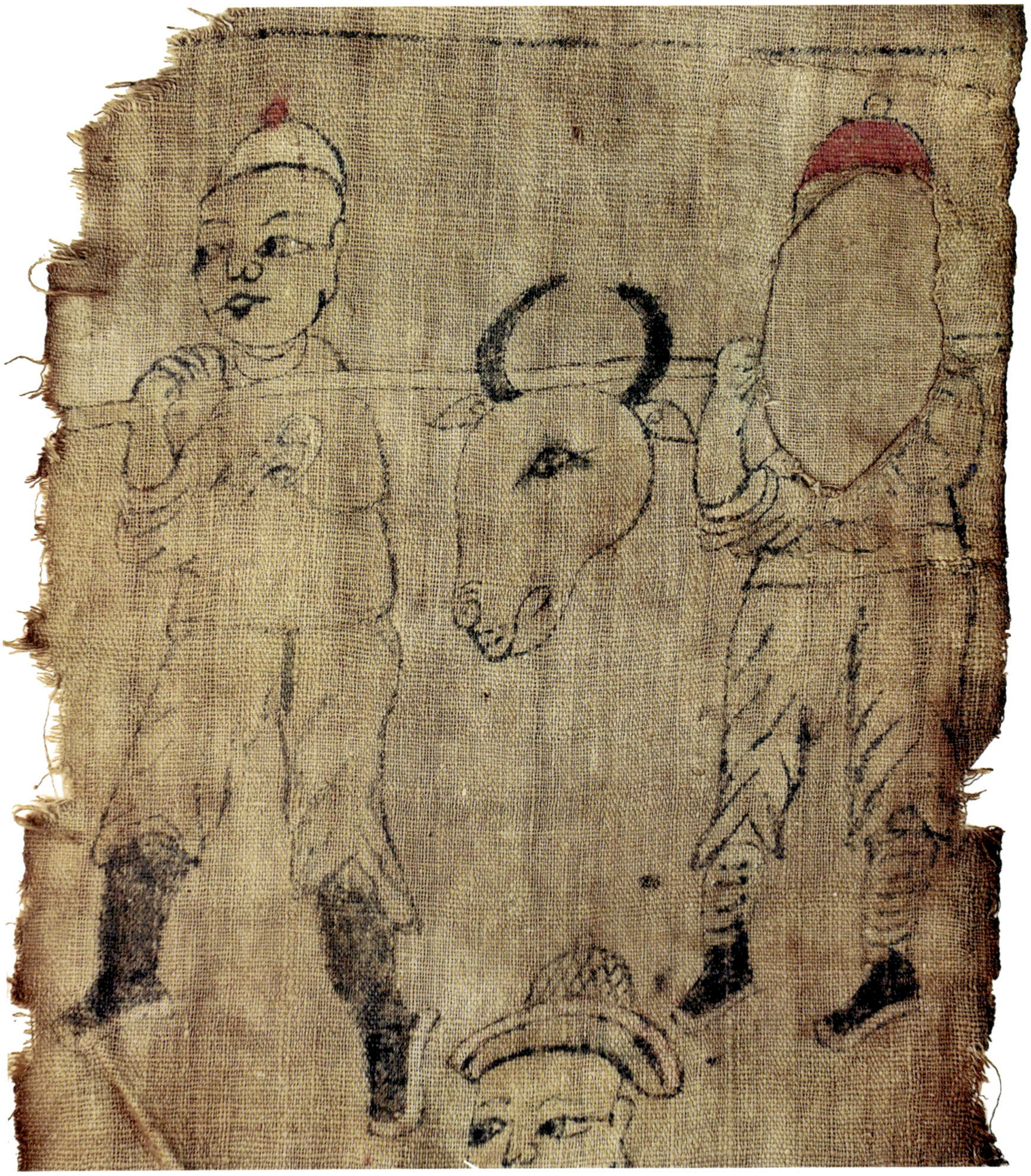

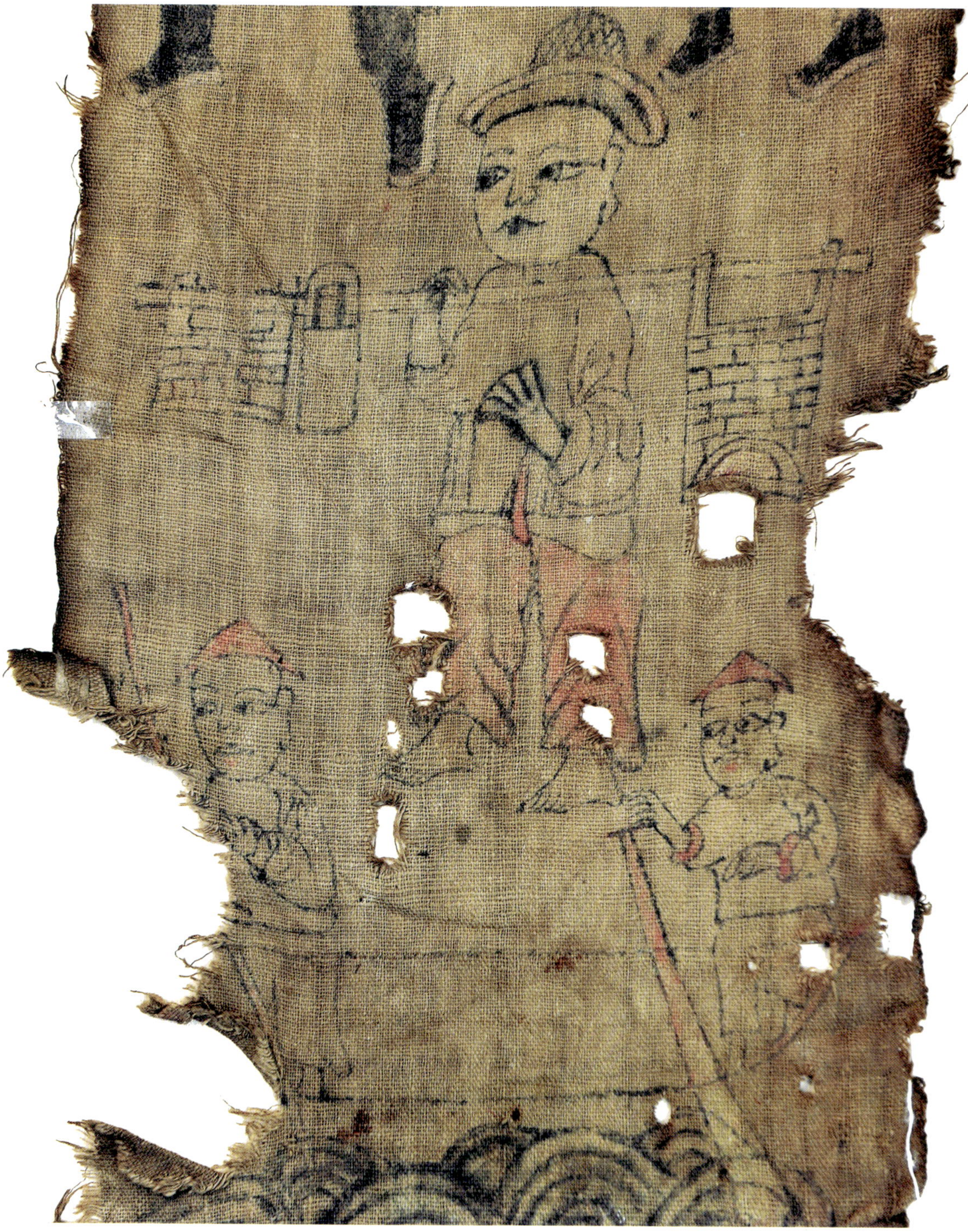

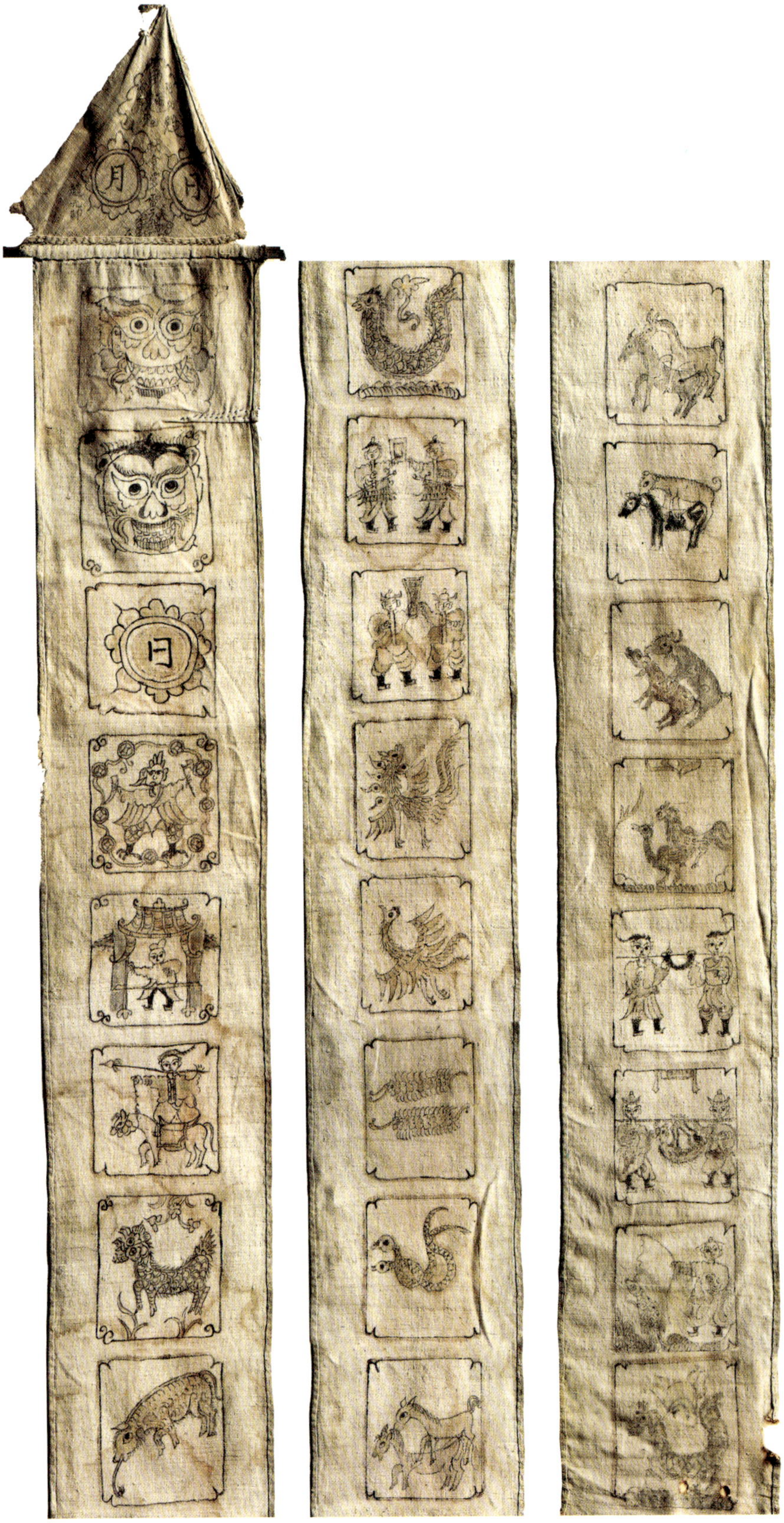

神图长卷（三）
年代：清代
尺寸：390cm × 22cm
收藏者：皇正光

月
日

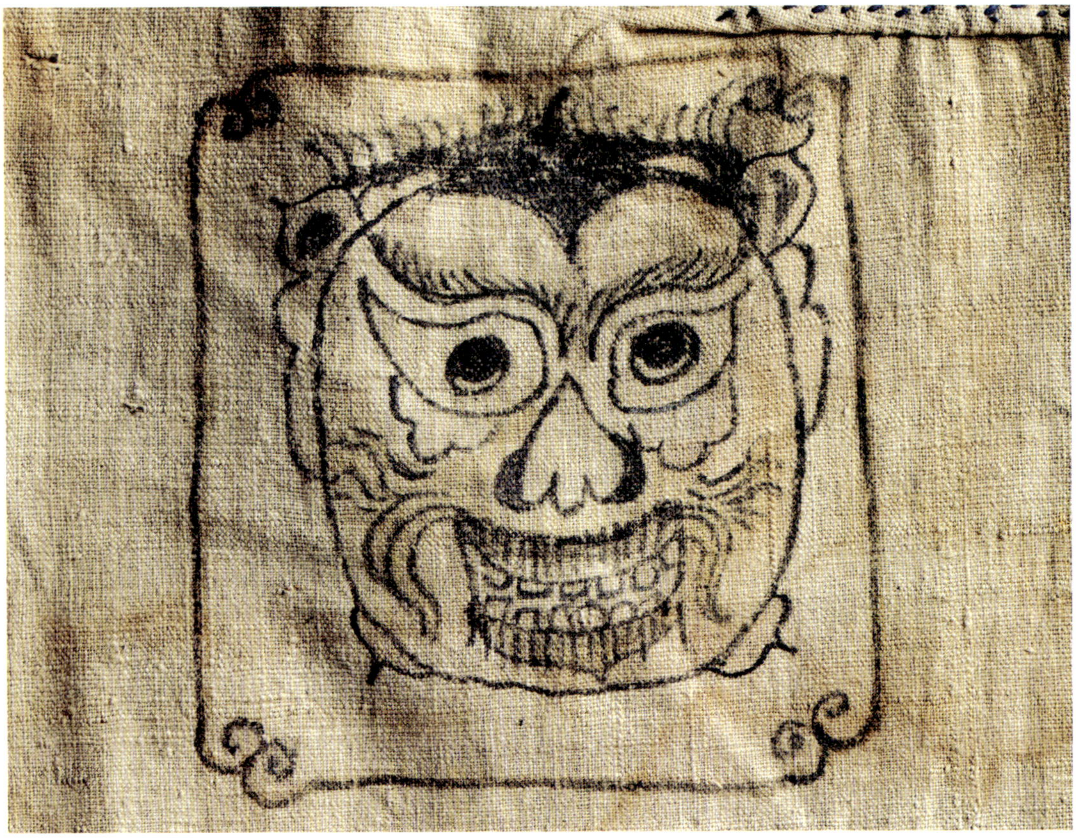

日

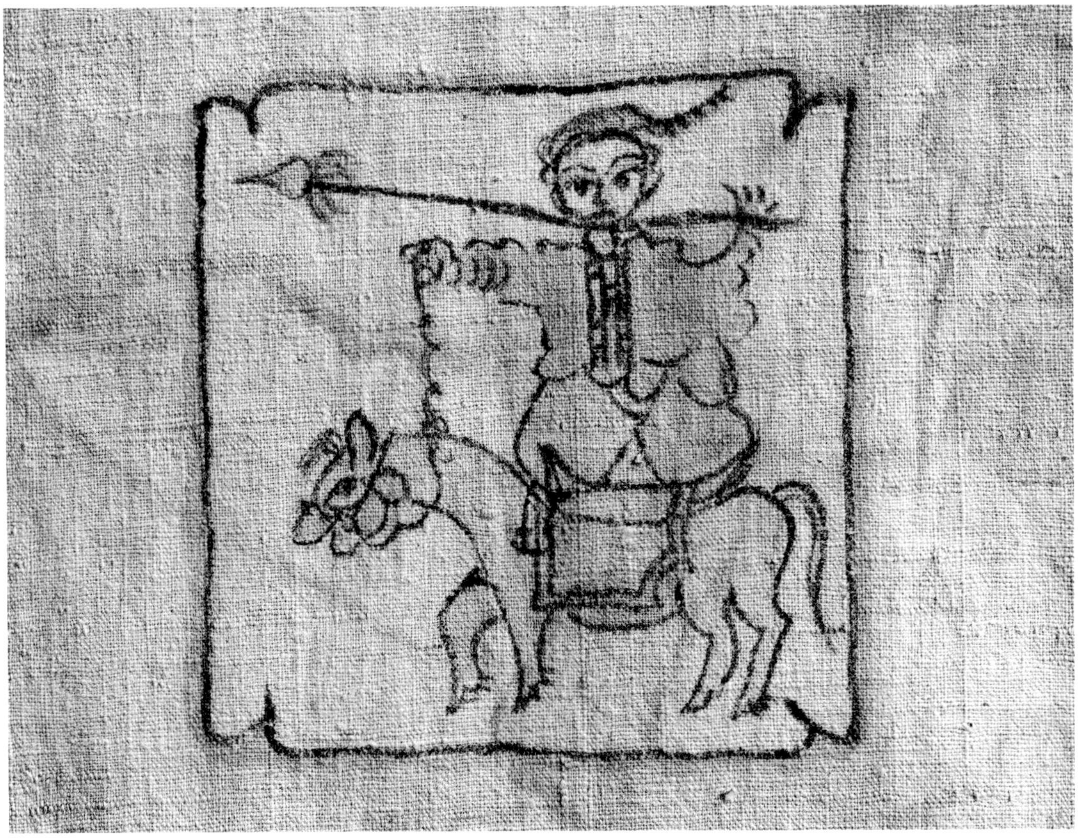

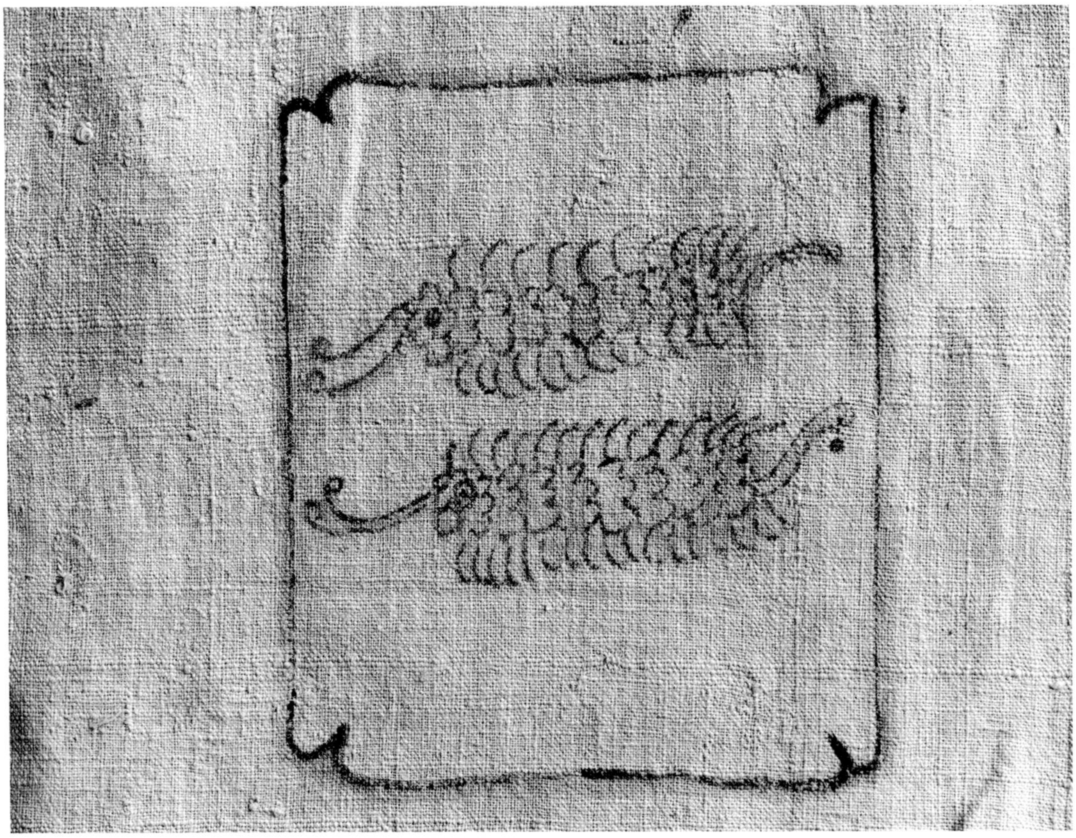

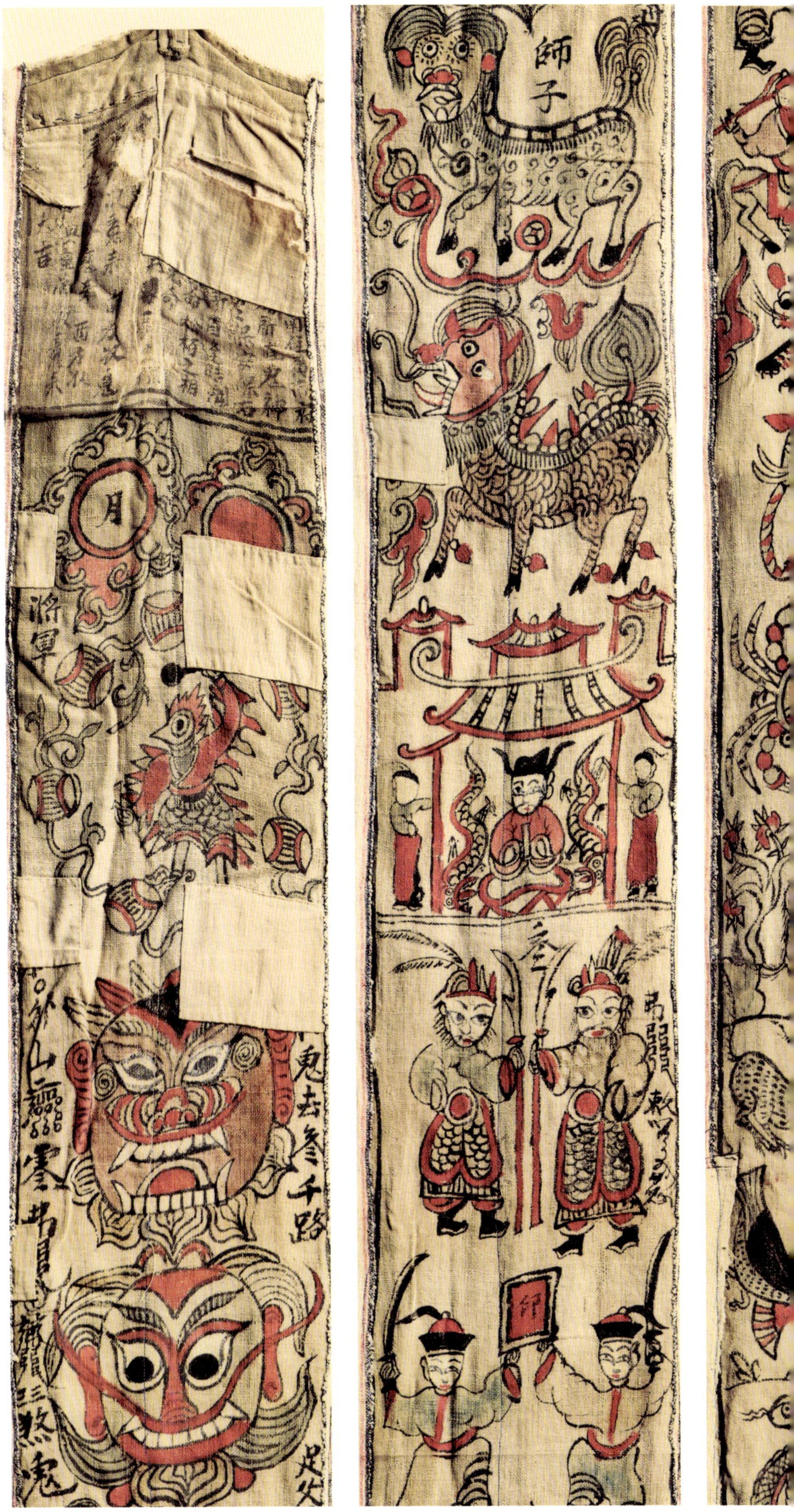

神图长卷（四）
年代：清代
尺寸：500cm × 23cm
收藏者：王寿光

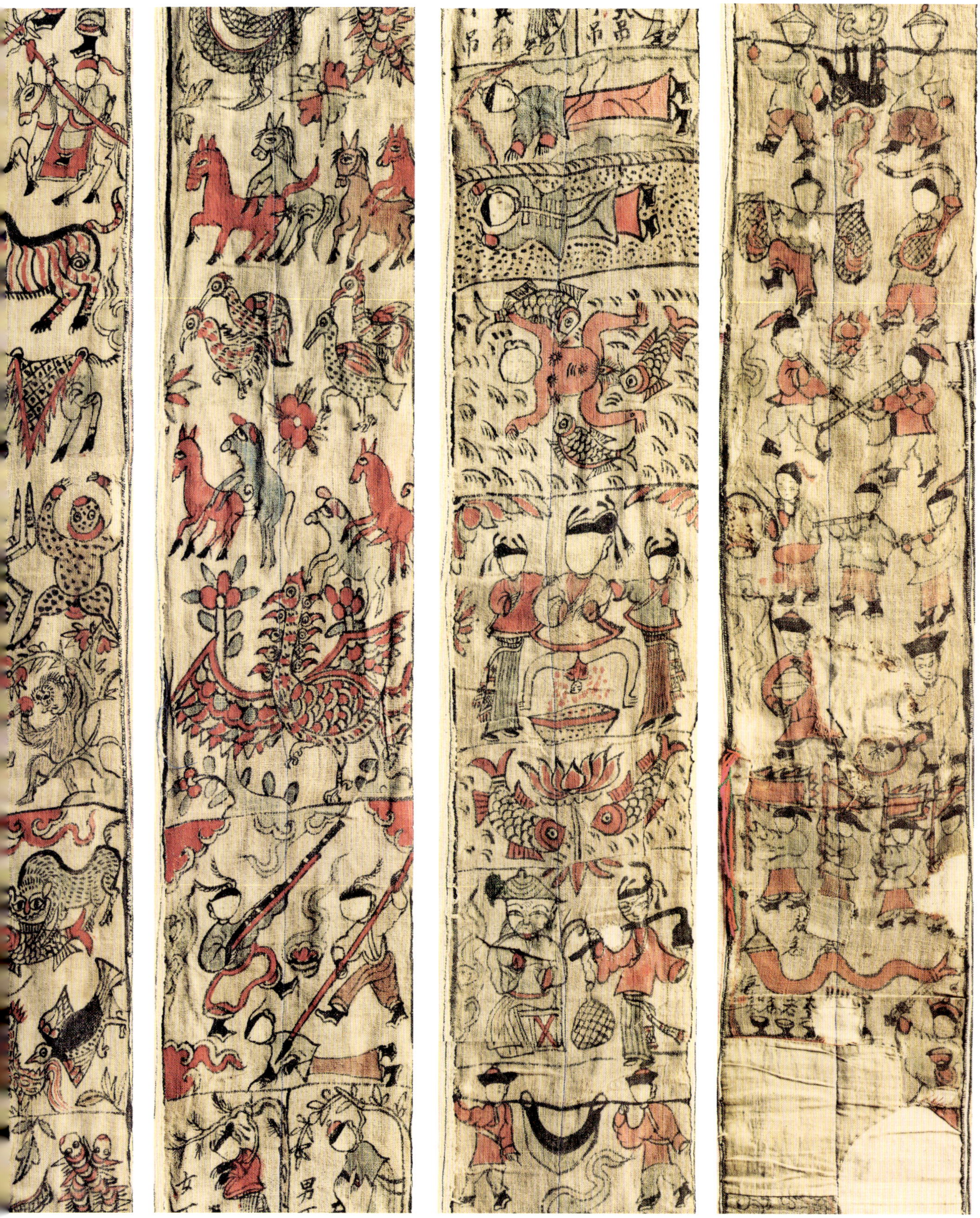

月

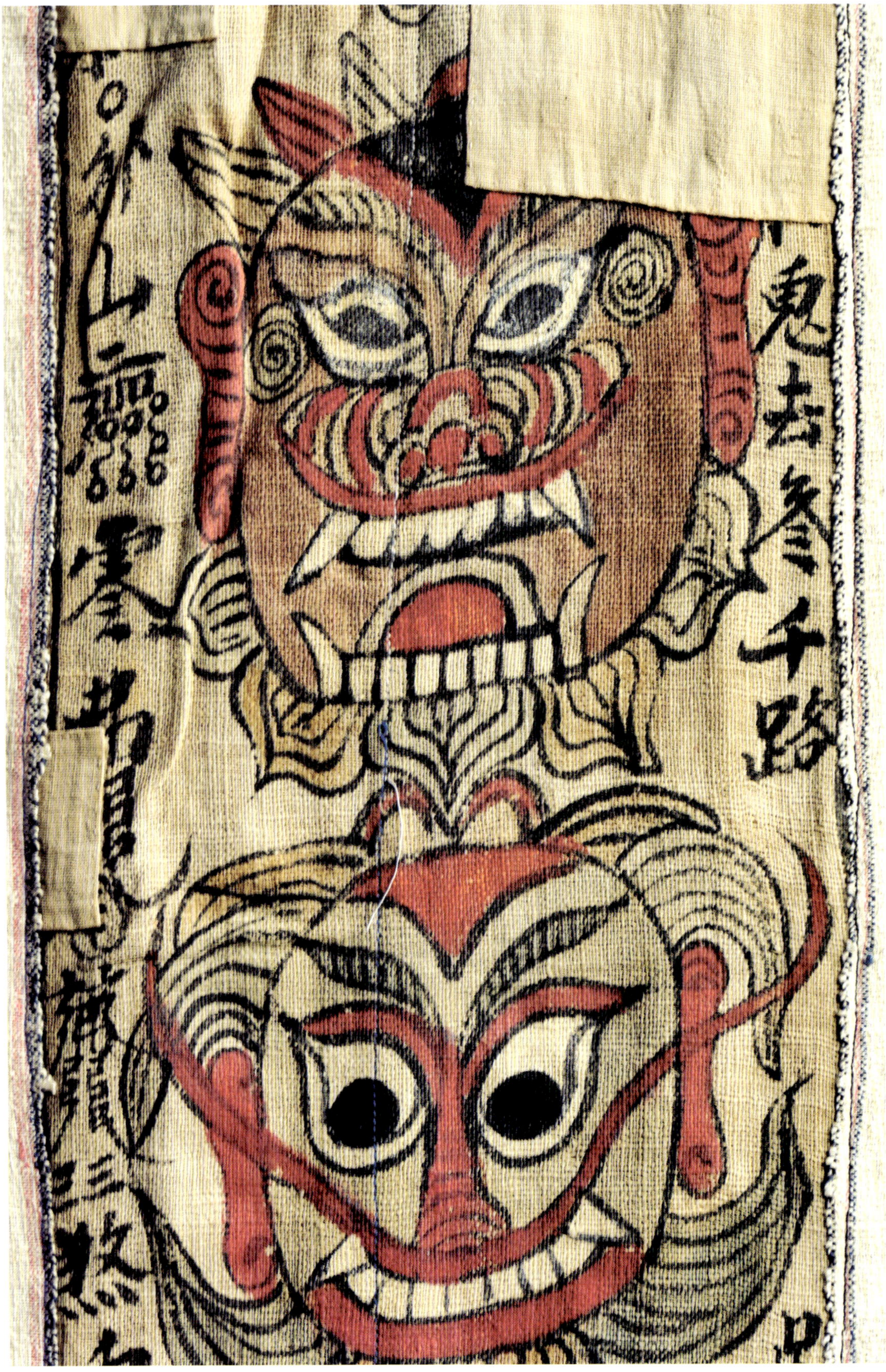
鬼去叁千路

師子

女丁吊
男丁吊

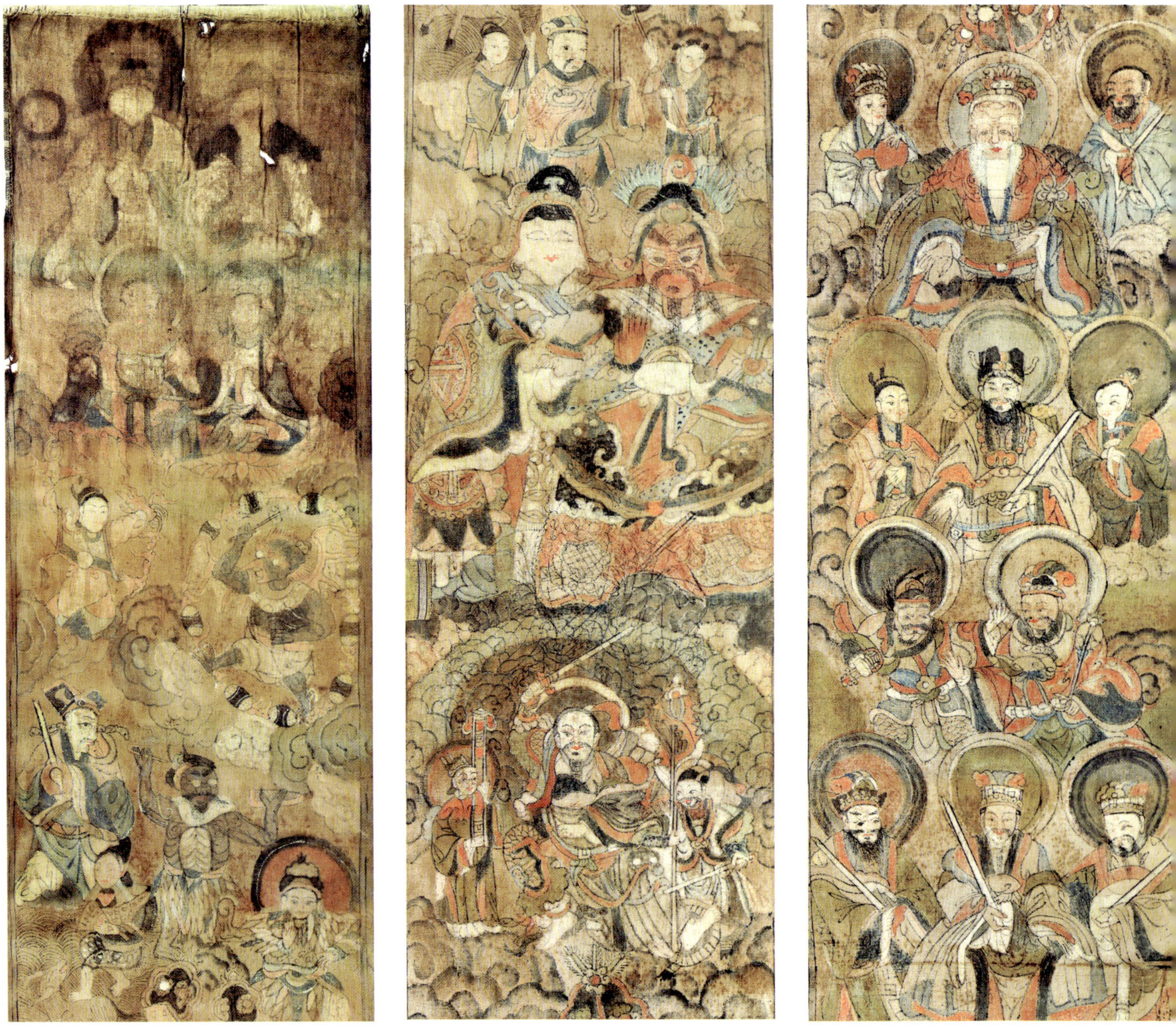

神图长卷（五）
年代：清代
尺寸：510cm × 26cm
收藏者：陆国斌

后记

我们长期从事云南少数民族古籍的抢救保护、翻译整理和出版规划工作，对云南少数民族古籍的分布、储量和传承现状有一个基本的了解，发现各民族都拥有或历史上曾经拥有过一些载体独特、形式各异的非纸质典籍，全面抢救保护、搜集整理这些分布零散、濒临消失且长期不被关注的少数民族非纸质典籍是一项具有重要意义的文化工程。

2015年初，我们便逐步对各民族的非纸质典籍开展专题调查，不断征集线索、采集古籍图片，随着资料的不断累积，便萌生了将非纸质典籍专题影印出版的想法。这个想法得到云南人民出版社的大力支持，经申报入选“国家民文出版项目库”，并获民族文字出版专项资金的经费支持，为编纂出版本书创造了有利的条件。2017年，本书主创团队参与云南大学周琼教授主持的国家社会科学基金重大项目“中国西南少数民族灾害文化数据库建设”，进一步推动了本项目的执行。

抢救保护承载着丰富民族文化内涵的云南少数民族非纸质典籍，具有重要的意义，也是一个充满挑战和未知的尝试。全面搜集云南各少数民族的非纸质典籍是一项耗时费钱费力的工作，这些典籍东一本西一样地散布在全省各地，从线索征集到一一获得授权采集图片确实经历了各种波折。

有的图片在采集过程中受自然条件的限制，采集难度较大。特别是金石铭刻类的图片，有的稍模糊，或缺乏全景图，甚是遗憾。图片如愿采集回来了，要将这些琳琅满目的典籍进行鉴别、释读、分类更是一项艰巨的任务，没有统一的划分标准可以参照、没有现成的经验可资借鉴，我们唯有摸着石头过河。进入统稿、编排环节，我们既要考虑覆盖云南各世居少数民族，又要考虑丛书的体量、编排等，取舍两难，着实让人困扰。最后，我们唯有以抢救保护、搜集整理少数民族古籍资料为出发点，以云南少数民族非纸质典籍的文化价值作为评判标准，以期为社会科学研究、文化产业发展等提供可资借鉴的材料。就收录范围，我们采用广义的民族古籍概念，适当突破民族古籍学学科的界定和范围，各民族的金石铭刻、骨刻、丝帛素书、竹木简牍等都是我们收录的对象，而结绳记事、刻木记事、树叶信等族属不明、内涵不清、争议较大的暂不作收录。所收录典籍的时间下线统一为1949年以前。就典籍的考释和图解，目前学界对各民族古籍的搜集整理、研究程度参差不齐，对古籍的翻译整理和释读等亦有巨大差距。如对纳西族非纸质典籍的收集、研究起步较早，我们基本可以释读典籍的名称和内容。但彝、壮、藏、傣等民族的非纸质典籍研究尚处于起步阶段，释读、命名尚有难度，如壮族的骨刻书，我们知道是用于历算的，但具体的内涵、使用方法尚未形成统一定论，我们实不敢妄解。所以部分非纸质典籍的文字说明略显简单粗陋。

本项目得到了云南人民出版社的大力支持和配合，特别是金学丽编审在项目策划、调研、稿件甄选、编辑等方面倾注了很多的心血，为项目的顺利开展做出了巨大的努力。吴贵飙馆长、普学旺译审、谢沫华研究馆员、起国庆研究馆员在项目申报、执行等方面给予了切实可行的指导意见和帮助。

本书资料的收集，得到丽江市东巴文化研究院、丽江市博物院、丽江玉龙纳西族自治县图书馆、文山壮族苗族自治州民族宗教事务局等基层民族古籍工作部门的全力支持和配合，得到李德静、牛增裕、木琛、李瑞山、王明富、和丽宝、赵庆莲、陆保成等专家的鼎力相助，谨致谢意。

为较好地呈现这套丛书，我们多方求证、全面搜集典籍、认真编排，确实做了很多切实的努力。但鉴于本书的执行、撰稿人员以青年学者居多，书稿难免有考虑不周和不当之处，敬请读者批评指正！

本书编委会

2018年12月

Postscript

We have been engaging in the rescue, protection, translation, sorting and publication planning of ancient books and records of ethnic minorities in Yunnan for a long time, and have a basic understanding on the distribution, reserves and inheritance status of ancient books and records of ethnic minorities in Yunnan. We find that all the ethnic minorities have or once had some non-paper ancient books and records with unique carriers and various forms in history. It is a cultural project of great significance to comprehensively rescue, protect, collect and sort out these scattered non-paper ancient books and records of ethnic minorities that are on the verge of disappearance and have not been drawing attention to for a long time.

We began to conduct special investigations on non-paper ancient books and records of various ethnic minorities, and are constantly collecting clues and pictures of ancient books and records since the beginning of 2015. With the continuous accumulation of data, we came up with the idea of photocopying and publishing special subjects of non-paper ancient books and records. This idea was vigorously supported by Yunnan People's Publishing House, and it was selected into the "national project library for publication of ethnic books and records" through application. Besides, it was also supported by the special fund for the publication of the ethnic books and records, and has created favorable conditions for compilation and publication of this book. In 2017, the creative team of this project participated in "the Establishment of the Database for Disaster Culture in the Ethnic Minorities in Southeast China" (Approval Number of the Project: 17ZDA158) which is the major project of the national social science foundation, and vigorously promoted the implementation of this series of books.

It is of great significance to rescue and protect the non-paper ancient books and records of ethnic minorities in Yunnan, which carries over rich ethnic cultural connotations, and is also an attempt full of challenges and mysteries. It is a time-consuming, costly and arduous task to collect all the non-paper ancient books and records of ethnic minorities in Yunnan. These ancient books and records are widely scattered all over the province. Relevant working personnel have experienced various twists and turns from collecting the clues to obtaining the authorization to collect pictures one by one. Restricted by the natural conditions, some pictures are difficult to take. In particular, the inscription pictures are slightly blurred or lack of panoramic images. What a pity! At last, the pictures were collected as expected. It is an arduous task to identify, interpret and classify these dazzling records. There is no unified classification standard to refer to and no ready-made experience to base on. We have to grope our way. In terms of compilation and arrangement, not only should we consider the coverage of ethnic minorities living in Yunnan, but also we should take the volume and arrangement of the series of books into account. It is really confusing to make choices. Finally, we can only take the rescue, protection, collection and sorting-out of the ancient books and records of ethnic minorities as the starting point, and the cultural value of non-paper ancient books and records of ethnic minorities in Yunnan as the evaluation standard, so as to provide reference materials for social science research and cultural industry development. In terms of the scope of inclusions, we adopt the broad concept of ethnic ancient books and records and appropriately break through the definition and scope of ethnic ancient books and records. Inscriptions, bone carvings, silk books and bamboo and wooden engravings of various ethnic minorities are all included in our collection scope, while the records of rope knotting, wood carving and leaf letters are not included for the time being due to their unclear and controversial connotations. The lower limit of time of the ancient books and records collected is uniformly fixed as prior to 1949. In terms of the interpretations and illustrations of ancient books and records, collection, collation and research on ancient books and records of various ethnic minorities are at different levels, and there is a huge gap in the translation, collation and interpretation of ancient books and records. For instance, due to early start of the collection and research on the Naxi non-paper ancient books and records, we can basically read names and contents of the ancient books and records. However, the research on non-paper ancient books and records of the Yi, Zhuang, Tibetan, Dai and other ethnic minorities is still in the initial stage, and it is difficult to read and name them. For example, we know that the bone carvings of the Zhuang Ethnic Minority are used for calendar calculation, but no unified conclusion has been reached on their specific connotation and method of use. We don't dare to make improper interpretations. Therefore, some of the explanatory notes on the non-paper ancient books are slightly simple and not so detailed.

This project has received vigorous support and cooperation from Yunnan People's Publishing House. In particular, Senior Editor Jin Xueli has spared no efforts in project planning, research, manuscript selections and editing, and made a great contribution to the smooth development of the project. Director Wu Guibiao, senior translator Pu Xuewang, Research librarian Xie Mohua and Qi Guoqing have provided practical guidance and help in the project application, implementation and other aspects.

Data collections for this book has been completely supported and cooperated by the Research Institute of Dongba Culture of Lijiang, the Library of Yulong Naxi Autonomous County of Lijiang, the Affairs Bureau of Ethnic and Religious Affairs of Zhuang-Miao Autonomous Prefecture of Wenshan and other grass-roots departments of ethnic ancient books and records. We would like to express our gratitude to Li Dejing, Niu Zengyu, Mu Chen, Li Ruishan, Wang Mingfu, He Libao, Zhao Qinglian, Lu Baocheng and other experts.

We have made lots of practical efforts in seeking confirmations from various sources, comprehensively collecting ancient books and records and making arrangements carefully, so as to better present this series of books. However, since the book is mainly collected and compiled by young scholars, it is hard to avoid making incomprehensive and improper considerations. We are looking forward to your criticism and corrections!

Editorial Board of the Book

December, 2018